LOST LETTERS FROM THE SEARCH FOR THE PERFECT WOMAN
A Jungian Perspective

BY

J. Grant Holm

and

Dr. Charles Goldsmith

In memory of Dr. Charles Goldsmith who often said: "Life is a mystery, not to be reduced to problems or issues, except by those who can't walk in the mystery"

PROLOGUE

She sits there on the hillside;

The wind blows through her soft brown hair

And gently lifts her silken skirt

To reveal more than she'd dare;

Her shapely body is true perfection

And arouses me at times,

But I have never seen her face;

So much beauty could destroy me.

Is she only imaginary?

But I know that she is real

And in her I can see

The best I have to offer;

We walk together hand in hand

And sometimes embrace,

But no wanton desires intrude

For we are both Heaven-bound.

INTRODUCTION

In his novel, "The Girl With the Golden Eyes," Balzac wrote the
following: "Last Thursday . . . I was strolling about . . . I found myself face
to face with a woman . . . This was no case of stupefaction, nor was she a
common street-walker. Judging from the expression on her face, she
seemed to be saying: 'What! You are here, my ideal, the being I have
thought of, dreamed of night and morning! . . . Take me, I am yours . . .'
And so on . . . So I looked at her closely. My dear fellow, from a physical
standpoint, this incognita is the most adorably feminine woman I have
ever met . . . . Ever since I have taken interest in women, my unknown <u>she</u>
is the only one whose virginal bosom, whose ardent and voluptuous curves
have realized for me the unique woman of my dreams . . . . She is the very
essence of woman, an abyss of pleasure whose depths may never be
sounded: the ideal woman."

One may wonder about the nature of these images projected here as the
"ideal" or "perfect" woman. Is this merely a haphazard projection onto an
external object? If it is not, what is the nature of the projection that elicits
these strong images of the perfect woman? One may be mystified by the
strong molding and shaping factor of the aesthetical tendency.
Consequently, the effect captivates one in an increasing aesthetic
experience, enchanted by a vision, in an ever extending space and an
immeasurable depth of time.

On the one hand, rational, reasoned elements appear to play no significant
role; they even seem to recede into a misty background of fantasies and
images when one encounters the perfect woman. On the other hand, there
is a tug at the strings of consciousness to understand, to explain, to analyze
what is happening to oneself when one meets his "perfect woman." Freud
was puzzled by this riddle as he called it. "Throughout history people
have knocked their heads against the riddle of the nature of femininity. . . .
Nor will you have escaped worrying over this problem, those of you who
are men; to those of you who are women this will not apply–you are
yourselves the problem."

In what is to follow, both elements will be found. The aesthetical
tendency to admire, to cherish, and even enshrine the "perfect woman"
will be reviewed as something outside the province of reason. At the same
time, an attempt will be made to follow the strands of the riddle, to bring

into consciousness, to understand, to explain, to the degree we are able, the patterns of the unfolding of the "perfect woman."

A few themes found in the writing need to be commented upon. First, Carl Jung has proposed that we all have the opposite inside. "That the complementary character is a fact which can no longer seriously be doubted." He proposes that a feminine woman has a masculine soul (animus), and a manly man has a feminine soul (anima). "If therefore, we speak of the _anima_ of a man, we must logically speak of the _animus_ of a woman." Whereas logic and objective reality commonly prevail in the outer attitude of man, or at least are regarded as ideal, in the case of woman it is feeling. But in the soul the relations are reversed: inwardly it is the man who feels and the woman who reflects.

Second, the concept of the projection needs our attention. Projection signifies a transmitting of a subjective process to an object. Looking for the perfect woman is a process of dissimilation, wherein the subjective content of a "perfect woman" is cast out of a man, and, in a sense, incorporated in a object, a woman, outside.

Thus, in projecting onto the "perfect woman," the man detaches a content (a feeling, for instance) from himself; he then transmits it to, therewith animating, the "woman" of his desire.

The following pages will allow the male reader to project from his inner content. They will allow the woman reader to understand the nature of the projection "put" upon her. These pages will allow one to follow the strands of the projection, plat the cord of understanding, and weave a fabric of appreciation of the "perfect woman."

It should be noted, however, that the structure of the book will quickly reveal the dichotomy between art and science. This is not a scientific expose, but rather a "poetic" approach that diverges from traditional form and organization. The interaction of various conscious and unconscious elements in life cannot be partitioned off neatly; each experience flows into the next. The following themes flow subtly, each developing into the next. Like the analytical discussions this work evolved from, the continuity is there, even if it is apparent only in retrospect.

    – Dr. Charles Goldsmith - May, 1982

August 12, 1953

My dear Son,

I know you may feel some shock and even possibly some anger at hearing from me after all these years, but no one can ever make up for a past filled with regrets. I do not ask for your pardon, nor do I forgive myself for abandoning you and your mother when you were too young to even remember. However, I was obsessed with a quest that I could not deny. I was seized with a burning torment that drove me on in search of the perfect woman. That is not to say that I did not love you or your mother, but something inside me demanded that I seek beyond the boundaries of love to the very ends of the earth to find something that may only be buried in the depths of my soul.

The very fact that I am bothering to write to you after all this time may make you think of me as arrogant or even a fool. But I ask that you do not judge me on either count until you have heard me out, for I do not even judge myself. Rather, with the risk of sounding arrogant, I like to think of myself as a new Moses. Not one who has done great deeds and led a nation, but as one who has traversed to a sacred mountain and discovered truths that were not yet carved in stone. What I have found, only you can assess its value. I have not been able to utilize it, probably due to the guilt I have carried with me ever since the day that I left both of you. However, now I want to give you something that is part of my life, my research, my observations, as a legacy. Use it as wisely as you would a true inheritance, an inheritance that I cannot give you as I am not a rich man in material things. What I have tried to give to you lies within the pages of the letters I am about to send you.

Do you know, son, that the average man will probably never encounter the perfect woman. The first reason is that she is so rare and the second reason is that she is so difficult to comprehend that you could meet her and never realize it because you may not be able to fathom the depths where such perfection lies. I feel that after many long years of study I can ferret out the falseness that passes as perfection and can expose it so that others, like you, will not be fooled and can proceed to the real task of uncovering the real ones.

Actually, I do have some reservations about telling you everything I know about such an immense subject as women. Someone once said something to

the effect that he would tell all he knew about women only when he had one foot in the grave and the other on a banana peel. I suspect that he knew more than he was willing to tell and had the wisdom to keep it to himself. Alas, my folly may shine brighter than my words.

I do not want you to think that what I am about to give you should be considered as an instruction manual. Think of it instead as a treasure map where you will find all the clues in bits and pieces and then put them together for yourself. It did not all come to me in one brilliant flash of inspiration, so do not expect it to be imparted that way either. Hopefully, what will come out of my writings to you will be insight into history, humanity, yourself and, of course, the perfect woman. So, my son, wherever she may be, may you someday find her.

Love,

Your Father

August 29, 1953

Dear Son,

As much as I hate to disillusion you, my son, "woman" is not synonymous with "sex"; which is to say that women are not just sex objects. Do not think that sex is not important or does not have a place in a relationship, but having it "on your mind" will repel any such perfect woman should you chance to meet her. She will sense it and steer clear. You, of course, will not see her perfection through preoccupation with sex and will miss her value. The perfect woman will not be a "sex bomb" and your preoccupation will only lead you to a woman with the same thing on her mind.

I do not want to give the impression that the perfect woman is sexless. Not at all. She is the only woman who is truly in tune with her sexual feelings and can express them fully in a range of nuances that would stagger the imagination. She knows what it is and can use it. But not as a weapon or toy. To her it is the ultimate experience of, in, by and for LOVE. She is not a prude about it either. She will try anything, but only within the framework of love and respect. Try to take from her and you will end up getting nothing. But, ironically, she will take what she wants--orgasms, that is. She has no hang-ups about pleasure and takes as many as she can. You cannot give her orgasms, though, because only she can decide when and how she will have them. It is her choice and she chooses frequently.

She will always be attractive. She will not necessarily be a great beauty, but she will be good looking enough to make you look twice. Remember, she is not just a sex object so do not judge by looks alone.

> Gentle lady, don't despair
> If you think your body's not perfect,
> For nowhere is it written
> That you must compare yourself
> To those more well-endowed;
> For who sets the standard?
> You don't have to follow the crowd,
> For you have a lovely face
> And intelligence that's far
> Beyond those you envy;

With compassion and elegant grace,
No one's as loving as you are;
So let me tell of my secret
About the truth that I have found:
If I love the total person
And sex is joining of two souls,
Then the soul is more important
Than the shell...that carries it around.

Love,

Your Father

September 9, 1953

Dearest Son,

Without trying to sound totally ignorant, I am going to give you a brief, biased evolutionary history of women. Please excuse my generalizations, for it is only the "essence" that counts. One Biblical account says that she was created from Adam's rib, but I think that is symbolical. Elsewhere in the Bible it says that God created them both equal, male and female, but somehow I suspect that He did create man first, realized his imperfections and then corrected it by making woman. Either way, fact or fantasy, women have been around as long as man--keeping him going in more ways than one. Be they nomadic wanderers, cavemen or neolithic lake-dwellers, prehistoric man owes much to women. They raised the children after bearing them, prepared the food, made the clothing, educated the young and, in all probability, were the mainstay of their culture, having the opportunity to pass on knowledge, custom, etc., to the youngsters much as it is today. Father went off to work; mother stayed home to work on and with the kids. But in a primitive hunting environment, all the cavewives huddled together and the group interaction was like a large nursery school. There, amid the work and diaper changing, was the real exchange of ideas, philosophy, and education. Papa, chasing the wooly mammoth, did not have time for discussing the pleasures of poetry, square roots, Bach and Beethoven while dodging the wounded creature or stalking sabertooth tigers.

Back at the cave, women were keeping a semblance of sanity intact, feeding the mind and soul along with the body. Man worked for his stomach and the group's; women had time to discover the heart. Women were the beasts of burden and even today, despite the lack of muscle development, can withstand more pain, work longer and harder than man, and complain less--on a comparative basis. It was not until agriculture came into existence that women got their first big break. They, of course, having developed it in the first place. Agriculture led to wealth, and that is what attracted man's fancy to it. It sure beat beating the bushes and woman could even do it so it must be easy. "Move over, lady, and let me show you how it should be done," he said. But after it was all done, what good is it? Why, leaving it to his children--first born son--and, by the way, how does he know who he is? Some ground rules better be set up. Women will now remain in the barracks and refrain from any fooling around. Naturally, sacking the neighbor's village did not count as fooling around. So now with wealth and family and estate,

woman found a home. She also became property. But with it she gained a personality. She was MY woman, that is how I can tell her apart from all the others and she was the one best able to have many children and work the hardest. No sleeping beauty yet. She came from huddling around a cave fire all the way to being the president's mother. She has evolved the most, been through more trials and tribulation and is still seeking her birthright--her identity. Soon she will have equality, but did she ever stop to think that maybe she has been SUPERIOR all along? I contend that it was women who painted buffaloes and other improvements on cave walls. They developed--and kept--the pigments that made it possible, even though some women paint themselves up like buffaloes today. But it was all towards improving beauty, either of self or surroundings. It is women who plant flower boxes and hang colorful curtains, not men. And even if they do not design all the fashions, they wear them to enhance their beauty and to salve men's vanity. She wears what he creates...and with his money. So women, in their striving for perfection, recognize that beauty is a primary concern.

Not having the natural display of say, a peacock, women make do with what they have and are clever at improving upon nature. But stripped of all the rouge, lipstick, hairspray, deodorant, and fingernail polish, women have a natural beauty that must be discovered. This beauty comes from within and is a quality of soul--not soul itself. It gives an indication of the quantity by its quality. One goes with the other and is dependent upon the other. The more soul, the more inner beauty. This is sometimes mistaken for personality, but it is not that. Personality can be developed, used like a tool or mask and can hide inner ugliness. Inner beauty is sincere, warm and enhanced by personality. But how does this beauty come about? It is the radiating of wholeness, essence of the being, individuation, etc. The word, "soul" will suffice. It contains four elements: thinking, feeling, intuition, and sensation. The balanced interaction of these four functions gives off a distinct character that can be felt by others. It is the genuineness, sincerity, warmth that one experiences when one encounters it in another being. Carl Jung called it individuation. Let me just call it inner beauty, soul power or whatever, no technical term will simplify perceiving it. But lest we lose sight of our original task of finding the perfect woman, let it be known that the "right" woman for you may not be perfect, for "right" and "perfect" are not the same in my context. You can be very happy with the right woman, but it does not necessarily mean that she has the perfection I am talking about. A lack of bad habits, or faults, does not mean perfect either. The difference between the right woman versus the perfect woman will become more

apparent when I tell you about the Lost-Soul theory as advanced by Plato and the "eggshell" theory.

So, son, getting back to inner beauty for a moment, what I wish to stress is that the beauty is there because it is not cluttered by ugliness. Sure, everyone gets angry, irritated, etc., at times, but what is absent is a negative attitude toward life that is very evident in the absence of such negative feelings as envy, hate, pettiness, etc. The beauty shines through because there are no dark clouds in the soul to hide it. This again is not an idealistic view. It does not imply that you are searching for a saint. The perfect woman can swear, get angry, hate something, show disgust, etc., but it is the appropriateness that sets it off from just plain negative feelings towards life. Just like when I previously addressed personality, I did not mean to imply a perfect personality. There will be and must be flaws if she is human. Likewise, the completeness or wholeness of the functions ("having it all together") is not to be taken literally. No one can be expected to achieve such an undertaking. It is a lifelong quest to reach that pinnacle, but the secret lies in the journey--the constant striving--rather than in the attainment. The perfect woman will never appear to be a Christ-like picture of goodness. That is unrealistic. What you hope to find is a woman with the soul of a goddess, the heart of a queen, the passion of a Helen, etc. Nowhere do I imply a religious overtone or super-morality. Who wants a moralizing woman who would never take a drink and proclaim that "lips that touch liquor will never touch mine"? The secret lies in moderation, in balance, in common-sense. She has a sense of the appropriateness and is able to read the feeling of the moment. Believe it or not, most women are fairly well adapted to feelings; it is their nature, although some can argue that a woman could have an undeveloped feeling function.

You may well question why I went back to prehistoric women to look at the evolutionary changes. So what if she has had to adapt through the ages? Well, the static quality, the unchanged portion, the spirit of woman is what reflects most in the soul. That, some feel, predates creation itself. The feminine principle of the soul is timeless. The important thing is that it is timeless and is shared by all women everywhere in all times. In as much as they are human and have physical characteristics, they all have certain feminine traits that cannot be altered, no more than men can bear children. Women have a set of feminine characteristics that are uniquely theirs: moods, for instance. A woman can use moods like a musician can use a piano. She can strike a note (mood) and if that is not to her liking, she will hit another

key (change her mood). A man is only plagued by moods. He neither understands them nor thinks he has any control over them and, actually, he does not. He is powerless. Moods have power over him. So there is a clear-cut difference between the sexes that cannot be legislated away. The same applies to personal relationships. Women are just more in tune to other people while men are more preoccupied with things and ideas. It is the woman in the family who reminds a man of his mother's birthday, sends out get-well cards, arranges parties, finds out the local gossip, etc. Outside of business, men are not very effective in the subtleties of relationships; even in business, women, as secretaries, are a necessity because men could not function without the feminine touch that they lack.

This feminine principle is important in dealing with the soul because it implies the presence of its opposite. Every woman has some of the masculine principle in her soul just as every man has some femininity in his soul. They are not mutually exclusive. The presence of masculinity presupposes the presence of femininity. The masculine element in women Jung called the animus while the feminine element in men he called the anima. They can be isolated for purposes of psychological and philosophical discussion, but in reality they are never found alone. That somewhat explains the choice of marriage partners, for other than getting caught up in projections, it is the unconscious striving to find the masculine/feminine balance that complements each other, just as in the complementing of personality types: the shy man marrying the vivacious woman. This masculine/feminine complementary mechanism I will further explain later when we get into the interaction of the anima and animus.

Love,

Your Father

September 21, 1953

Dear Son,

    I am now going to jump right into the Lost-Soul theory. This goes back to the time of Plato, as found in his "Symposium," and probably predates that era by the very fact that it was first recorded then. Who knows for how many eons it was passed on by legend. Be forewarned, though, that what I am about to set forth is only a theory and should be taken with a grain of salt. Read it as though it is only ancient humbug, not a myth that is viable today. And after reading it, do not feel compelled to try to set sail on a grand and glorious quest. The anima has the power to wreak havoc in one's life and this is an area that is her territory. So heed my warning....

    Once upon a time, as the ancient Greek philosophers would have us believe, human beings were not in the form they are now. They were originally created male and female in one entity--like a man and woman fused back-to-back. As a race, they became too smart and powerful for their own good and were about to assault the gods and take over. The gods perceived this threat and to punish them and/or render them helpless, divided each being in half. That means that there were twice as many humans, but half were male components and the other half female, rather than one happy "unit." They then spent their time--instead of plotting against the gods--trying to seek out the original other half from which he/she had been separated. True happiness could not be achieved until each half was re-united with its original "missing" half. So everyone spent their time searching for the other half of their long, lost soul. The end.

    It is a funny little story is it not? Is there, somewhere out there, the other half of your long, lost soul? That there is just one "someone" out there who, if you could find her, would make you happy foreverafter?

    A myth is not an old, forgotten, ancient story. It is about our history and our present and our future. It may be symbolic, but its truth can be felt. The funny little joined humans may be only a fantasy, but the essence of the story is part of us all. So how do we cope with such a situation? How do we find happiness despite our failure to find our "missing half"? Enter the "eggshell" theory. I do not know where or how it developed, but of necessity, it offers consolation if not a solution. The eggshell theory goes one better on the original lost-soul myth. Confronted with the prospect that you may never

find your missing half (when I say missing half, I mean for a man the complementing woman and for a woman, the man. Simply put, the missing half is always the opposite sex, the one who is really "right" for you) what do you do? Do you search all your life to try to find it, or do you just settle for whatever you can get even though you know it is not the missing half?

Being practical, you take what you can. But it is not a perfect fit, not really the one and only missing half. Yes and no. Perfect no, but a fit, yes. If you were to break an egg in half, you could put the empty shell halves back together and see that they fit perfectly. If you were to break a dozen eggs in half and mix up the empty shells and then try to match up the two original halves by trial and error, you would find that in the end they all match up exactly with the two original halves always going back together. But in your trial and error of matching up the 24 empty shell halves, you found that some fit almost exactly, but not quite, and some just did not match up even close, while some were in between. The analogy is obvious and is just the way life is. Some, on a trial and error method, find the perfect or right mate. Some do not even match closely and the majority are in between--they mesh close enough that they can be happy enough about it. So if you found a mate that was close to you in temperment, intellect, etc., you could be happy enough and not willing to risk the chance of continuing to look for someone better. That is how most of the world does it. Few are fortunate to land a perfect fit and a few--which is seemingly becoming the greater number--find a bad fit and end up calling it quits. The eggshell theory works fine as long as no one really believes in the lost-soul theory.

But even with all this theorizing, I want to stress one point: even if you found the missing half of your soul, that does not mean that it is perfect. The woman who is your missing half--or who completely complements your personality--is not necessarily a perfect woman. "Right," then, as I have said before, does not have to equate to "perfect." But if you could be happy with this right fitting, other half of your soul, why continue to search for the perfect woman? Hopefully, I will have answered that question before I am all finished....

Love,

     Your Father

October 6, 1953

My dear Son,

I do not know about you, but most of the books I have read lately about women are written by someone with M.D. or Ph.D. written after their name. As if that is the only qualification for having knowledge. But strangely, most of those books deal with only one aspect of her: sexuality. They try to dissect women very methodically, as if the right words, the right setting, the right touch, etc., will lead to perfect sex. They then analyze the orgasm and the sensations. I have yet to find where they address her moods, temperament, feelings, hopes, dreams, etc. It is all body. Where is her soul when all this is going on? Is the spirit out to lunch when the orgasm begins? I wonder if anyone realizes that some women do not need sex the same way men do?

Because of their different temperament and basic disposition, women respond differently than men to sex as most of the technique manuals point out, but they never tell you why. They break it down into foreplay, orgasm and afterglow like three rinse cycles in a washing machine. I have yet to find where someone points out the three levels of involvement. A woman experiences orgasms with her whole being, not just with her whole body. It is pervasive. Sex is an act of creation. Some women have reached the point where sex is an ego expanding experience and they know how to respond, thereby increasing their energy level. Many find satisfaction in little creative things men never comprehend. Such women get satisfaction out of simple creative tasks such as cooking and sewing or, if she is not tending a family, her job. So by gathering a little satisfaction here and there all day long, she does not need to hop into bed to have a gigantic orgasm to put all her frustrations to rest. But when she does experience an orgasm, be it one or many--by her choice--it encompasses her body, mind and soul. The total psyche gets involved, not just the brain sending back pleasure signals. Actually, an orgasm exists only in the mind. The sex organs do not sense pleasure; the brain directs it, or orchestrates the entire symphony, from the podium inside the head. But be that as it may, when the orgasm arrives, it affects the total being. On the physical or body level, there is a sense of satisfaction--relief of tension. This is a sensation that is transmitted by the body the same as hunger is relieved by food. The imagination and emotions--the second level--find gratification. There is a consciousness of pleasure, a relief of anxiety, a realization above and beyond what the body says. The last phase or third level involves the soul. A sense of fulfillment

is experienced as existential loneliness and despair are momentarily transcended.

Only when all three levels have been reached is there a sense of well-being, a "good feeling," a positive and meaningful experience.

Love,

Your Father

October 14, 1953

Dear Son,

I would like to bring up an entirely different subject: women and drinking. They do not mix. Never drink when women are around. You may say or do something foolish and even if you think that they are drunker and will not remember, they will. And it will come back to haunt you. Actually, being drunk, or just a little, will lower your inhibitions in dealing with women, but in the long run will be detrimental. Alcohol does lower your performance level in bed. Drinking is a good way to avoid sex.

Women can be sneaky. But the perfect woman does not have to resort to that. She is always in command so there is no need for her to be false. If she wants to go to bed with you, she will tell you so in so many words, or actions, depending on the circumstances. And if you understand her and can communicate openly with her, she will never have to resort to seduction. But on the other hand, if you get to the point where you gain self-knowledge and knows women and can withhold projections, there is no woman in the world who could seduce you no matter how hard she tried. That is, of course, unless you let her. And sometimes it is fun to resist just enough to see how hard she tries. But the perfect woman will not get caught up in those games. You will have to deal with her face to face as an adult in a relationship stripped of all those ploys. The lady knows what she wants and how to get it and usually along the lines of least resistance. She has character. And as Goethe said, "Character is nurtured midst the tempests of the world."

While I am on the topic of seduction, let us zero in for a closer look. Women are very aggressive. Usually they will be patient and give a man enough time and rope to hang himself--fall into her trap, that is--but occasionally a man will miss his cue or just bungle the whole thing. Then the mating game takes a turn for the better (or worse?). The woman is then forced to grab the reins and bring things back onto track. She will then be the initiator and lead the dance.

If a woman wants a man badly enough, practically nothing on earth can stop her pursuit, even if he is already married. She has three courses of action: one, seduction; two, showing affection; or three, pushing for a divorce. The first is individual in nature; she will seduce one somehow, usually striking (or appealing) to one's weakest spot. However, I think that

it is all a matter of determination and guts, coupled with social skills. Some women could not seduce a stranded sailor on a deserted island. Not because they did not want to, but because they just do not have the old-fashioned knowledge about how to use the feminine wiles and the confidence in themselves to pull it off. Many women today are ignorant of the ways in which a woman can or should appeal to a man. I fault the education system that stresses sex education as if once that is known, there is nothing else a woman needs to attract a man. It is as if that is her jar of honey and all she has to do is open it to attract all the males buzzing around her. And, unfortunately, with all that has gone the sense of modesty for many women. If she resorts to affection, she will try to win one with love. Likewise, if necessary, she can and will give all the reasons why you would be better off with her. On a positive note, she will not mention the reasons why you may not be better off.

However, never, never, push her to the point where she has her back against the wall. The laws of nature are very explicit here. You never corners a wild animal--the same goes for a woman--although they like pushing men into a corner to watch them squirm. If a woman is cornered, she has three alternatives open to her. First, she can run away. She will disappear out of avoidance and will vow never to let that happen ever again. In short, you will never see nor hear from her again. Second, if she is strong willed and has real spirit, you will hear from her again in some fashion. She will get revenge. You will not see the wrath of God because you will be too busy experiencing it. We have all heard about a woman scorned...so beware. Lastly, if cornered, she may revert back to "a little girl." That is, emotionally she may react in the same fashion she did when she was a child in encountering her father. She will regress to the point where she will view you as a father figure and react accordingly. And that interferes with trying to carry on an adult relationship. If, however, all you want to do is incur her wrath and not necessarily push her into reacting as if she were being cornered, you can do a very effective job by simply telling her that you can "read her like a book." Just tell her that you know more about her than she knows about herself. Such arrogance on your part will definitely evoke a response--a very negative one.

How would the perfect woman react to the preceding? (React is not the proper word, because the perfect woman does not react, but responds.) First, she has herself put together to the point where she does not have to play games and can spot them a mile away. She is secure and well-balanced,

internally, and would view seduction as a waste of time. If you are not in her league, or on her wave length, she is not going to lower herself to your level. Nor does she have to resort to such methods for if she wants something she will just ask and can accept the outcome of the reply. Can she be affectionate, loving? Like she invented it! Only she can express real love because she knows what it is and it is a part of her nature. She can use her resources appropriately. Love is her territory, so if you are not an expert, and sincere, she will lose you at the first turn.

Would she push someone into getting a divorce? That again is beneath her. She may help you to think your situation out and see it clearly, but she has no need to manipulate anyone and would not even want to involve herself with influencing any decision. She knows that if things turned out badly after a divorce, or there were any regrets, that she would be the target of blame and will not put herself into a position where she could be blamed. Could you push her into a corner, put her under pressure, get her into an uncompromising situation? No way. There is nothing you could find to use against her. She is not concerned with public opinion, so whatever you think might be embarassing to her has long since been forgotten by her. But the impossibility of getting her back against the wall lies in the fact that she cannot be manipulated or coerced. She is frank and outspoken and when necessary she can put you down before things get too far. The right word at the right time will defuse your threat and send you crawling into a corner. But that does not happen very often, only as a last resort, because she is tactful enough to parry any ploys before they even get started. And she is mature and intuitive enough to avoid anyone who would be so presumptuous as to believe that they could corner her in the first place.

Love,

Father

October 26, 1953

My Dear Son,

Before I continue on, I want to make one final point about the difference between the "right" woman and the "perfect" woman. There is another distinction to be made. I said before that the "right" woman may not be the perfect woman for you. Well, the reverse is also true. The perfect woman may not be right for you at some point in time. You could have a perfect woman and she could outgrow you, or you could find a perfect woman when you are not ready for her, mature enough, or appreciative enough. A woman when she reaches her "childing" stage is interested only in having children. She will choose a man at that point for the purpose of having a family, even though she may not love that man. Many times the man she chooses to give her children will also become her child. She is in her "childing" stage and when child rearing is past, she may move on to her "loving" stage; but the man who gave her children may no longer be right for her. She has, in this case, outgrown the circumstances, the stage, or driven him away by then. At that point, the right man once no longer is the right man. So, on the other hand, she is no longer the right woman, even if perfect. Time changes things sufficiently so that what was the right woman yesterday may not be the right woman today and vice versa. The world is in a state of flux and human nature is not static. Ever changing, evolving, growing, paths cross...like stars. We are each our own little heavenly body wandering around this earth like so many galaxies in the universe. But what about that magnificent star, that bright and ever shining glorious light so sought after by many--the virgin.

Many skeptics will say that there is no such a thing as a virgin in this day and age and I am almost tempted to agree with them. But I know better. Virginity is a strange thing and difficult to describe and understand. When I was in college many years ago, a friend once remarked that his mother was so ignorant that she still thought she was a virgin. Well, many years later, reflecting back, he could have been right. Virginity is not a lack of experience or sexual activity; it is a lack of knowledge and understanding. Some women, after an entire lifetime of sexual experiences may still be virgins because they never developed or understood their own sexuality. They may have had children, but never grasped the meaning of it, never valued it and thereby never formulated any feelings about their sexuality. For all practical purposes they were psychologically untouched.

Their bodies went through the act of intercourse, but their psyches never got involved. To lose their virginity, then, is not an act; it is a realization. Some will disagree, but what we are concerned with here are not dictionary definitions or moral standards, but with psychological truths which are often complex and contradictory.

Love,

Father

November 11, 1953

Dear Son,

In an earlier letter I briefly mentioned that in every woman there is a bit of masculinity and in every man a bit of femininity. This inclusion of the opposite nature in every person is called the anima in a man and the animus in a woman. The anima, a man's feminine component, is a constellation of power. It is a complex in so far as it manifests itself as a collection of female images, including those that go back to the beginning of time. If the female image ever existed, it is reflected in a man's soul-image, his anima. She does not have only one form, but an infinite number of reflected images. The anima can be thought of as a miniature woman living somewhere inside. Picture her, if necessary, as a real-live woman running around inside. However, the more abstract you can be, the better.

For some men, this will be an image of only their mother, or a mother, as this may be the extent of their exposure to femininity. For others it may include early encounters with a prostitute, so now it expands to encompass a Mother image and a Prostitute image. For those who have not developed beyond this stage, some analysts refer to it as the prostitute-Madonna complex. Actually, it is more developed than that for most men because they had encounters with sisters, aunts, grandmothers, sweethearts, and wife. These are also anima images even if they seem undeveloped. Other images include witch, princess, priestess, Amazon, shrew, seductress, little girl, fairy godmother, etc. This list, as I said before, is endless.

Mostly, to get a clue to what images you are harboring, watch for female dream figures. These most often are the anima appearing in different roles, or images, in dreams. There is no one set image as the anima is like a chameleon, changing forms constantly as she sees fit. The anima can be thought of as having a personality of her own, although in theory she does not have a true personality as such, but a cluster. The anima, as it shows itself as a complex, empowers the ego with energy such as love, creativity, recognition of beauty, etc. It is most important to remember that the anima plays an important part in all love, including sex.

A man cannot love of and by himself; it is the anima who allows it or wills it. If she decides to withhold her energy, her power, a man may be incapable of love. Therefore, it can be concluded that love is feminine in nature. All

women are capable of love as it is inherent in their soul. In a man, the anima, or carrier of the soul, is the necessary catalyst for love. If the anima is angry, she can and will withhold love, even creativity. Remember what I said about her having a personality of her own. She also has the power to wreak havoc in your personal relationships and life, bring down upon you physical and emotional illnesses and even drive you to destruction. You can begin to see her power and how necessary it is to have a good relationship with her. If there are any doubts, look in any hospital or on skid row and you will see evidence of her destructive nature--once again the woman scorned. Too many men go on throughout their life not knowing that she even exists, thereby not heeding her, or falling victim to her will. How much misery has the world known because of the ignorance of this one essential element in life?

As much as she represents hell and can create misery, she alone is the link between God and man and as such--as guardian angel--can bring you happiness beyond your wildest expectation. To keep from confusing her with a real woman, I will interchange, as the explanation deems, the term anima with "inner woman" as opposed to "outer woman"--the former being the little lady within and the latter being a flesh and blood physical woman.

How do these images come about; how are they developed? In the anima is the inherent existence of all possible feminine images. The earliest encounter a man has is that interaction with the mother. These prior images flow through the ego to the mother and back to add more images to the anima. The next time, the images plus the Mother image flows through the ego and gets projected onto woman A. Back goes the image of woman A to add to the collection of anima images. Then all of the internalized images, including the Mother image and woman A, gets projected onto woman B, etc. Each time the projection is made material is added to the anima. All this projecting is unconscious for we are constantly projecting. We also project only that which is unconscious and hence unknown to us.

Hopefully, what we project is correct, not like projecting a Prostitute image onto a woman who is not and then treating her as if she were one. Projecting can be simply defined as seeing a woman and saying to yourself, "She looks like she might be a prostitute," or "She reminds me of my sister" and then projecting the Prostitute image or Sister image onto that woman and treating her (relating to her) as if she were a prostitute or your sister. It is relating to another person through a preconceived notion--having the image in our mind

as to what we think they may be or would like them to be and then relating to them as if it were so. Most men, 99% of the time, project the wrong image mainly because the anima tells them to project the wrong image. She likes to play games like that where she can get you all fouled up and then sit back and laugh at your stupidity. That is referred to as an anima trick. Some men, or most, who are unaware of their anima and the infinite images, project the anima incorrectly and look for an ideal that is not suited to them. Their anima remains unconscious and hidden, so they do not know what they are projecting and end up finding a woman who can carry the images of what may well be the worst side of their nature.

What is known about the inner woman? She is the source of creativity. She has an independent personality and all the attributes of an outer, or real, woman. She can possess you and then you becomes an inferior woman or are plagued by bad moods. She can become angry and cause you to lose your creativity--also your sexual powers (much impotency can be linked to these dynamics). When she is the source of love, she empowers you with her energy. She is the go-between from the conscious to the unconscious. She will play tricks, but if you have a good relationship with her, even her tricks will be beneficial.

Back to the subject of love, because it is of paramount importance in dealing with inner and outer women. Consider the following: if the inner woman is the source of creativity and beauty and the center for all feminine traits, and since love is similar to creativity, especially in the form of motherly love, (and also that many aspects of love seem to be feminine in nature: tenderness, affection, etc.) then it's safe to assume that the inner woman is also a source of love in a man. When this happens, men do not really love in and of themselves, but through their inner woman. Then in order to love, a man must be possessed by his anima or no expression or feeling is forthcoming. Like creativity, the expression and feeling is through the anima. If so, then it is a man's inner woman reaching out for the outer woman--likes tending to attract likes. If this is so, then it is like a relationship between an inner psychic female and an outer physical female. However, to carry it one step further, it is really a pull of opposites for the inner woman is really seeking out a relationship with the inner man (animus) of the outer woman. Thus the love we feel is really the unconscious attempts of our inner opposite nature to unite. The physical aspects are between flesh and blood man and woman, but the psychological aspects of love are between their inner opposite components. It is the inner woman of a man responding to the

inner man of the woman and, therefore, consciously we have no control over our love "objects." If this is true, that this all transpires on an inner level, then there seems to be something to Plato's theory about two souls seeking each other out. The paradox is that if it is the inner woman who empowers us with love, then it is us who loves, but it is not really us because it is all unconscious: the ego did not make the choice. It is our anima who channels the love through us. She is the receiver and the giver. She receives it through the unconscious and give it to us consciously in the form of a possession. How is this then carried over into the realm of sex, remembering that sex is the highest expression of love there is?

When you are in bed with an outer woman, where is the inner woman? What is she doing? What is she thinking? If the assumption is true that the inner woman is the source of love and you are possessed by the inner woman when you love, then when in bed, you are also possessed by the love that comes from the anima and is empowered by her with sexual energy. Therefore, in your physical love-making with an outer woman, what is really taking place on an internal (psychological) level is the gratification of the inner woman. She is not capable of physical sex herself, so she shares it vicariously. The physical relief is between the outer persons, but the psychic gratification is between the inner opposites. So in effect, by giving of herself, empowering you with love, she makes it possible for you to find sexual satisfaction and by doing so, she received back satisfaction also, even if it is only in knowing that the love she created, or inspired, fulfilled its ultimate purpose.

I do not think that I can stress enough the importance of the anima and the traits of the anima or inner woman. A man's first experience with a woman is his mother. She is kind, gentle, loving, yet again she can be unloving and hurtful. It is this early uncertainty or unpredictability that give us the impression that woman can be a trickster. The inner woman is a trickster. She will cause you to do crazy things like going up and asking a girl for a date only to get a slap in the face. She will also try to possess you with a mood. This will cause you to be unable to feel or value. She can also be very jealous, thinking that she will be displaced by an outer woman and can even drive a wedge in a marriage to force the wife out. She is the source of creativity; she must be busy and needs an outlet to express herself.

The first thing you must do with the inner woman is recognize her, know what she does, how she plays tricks. The second step is to get to know her,

relate to her. You can reason with her just as if she were an outer person, but not necessarily by using logic on her. You must guard against falling on her side of the fence, so to speak, or she will possess you. (Possessions take the form of good and bad. Love is a good possession, as is creativity. Possessing you with a mood is bad.) She is the go-between from the conscious to the unconscious. She is the provider of intuition for a man.

You can communicate with your anima. Jung called it active imagination. If you are not at a point in life where this is a necessity, to understand the anima completely, it is best to leave well enough alone as she could lead you very much astray. Two dangers are ever present: the first is trying to know the inner woman before you are ready, before she is ready to reveal herself. The other is not knowing that she is ready to be made conscious and ignoring her. The first case will only result in an exercise in futility where she will make you look foolish. The latter, if not heeded, will bring you to your knees. The anima, as the soul-image and guardian of the unconscious, will force a man to see her, to reflect inwardly, usually by slowing him down with a serious illness or something. That slows him down so as to have the time to put his house in order and get get acquainted with the lady from the other side who will guide him through the labyrinths of the unconscious... before it is too late.

Love,

Father

November 19, 1953

Dear Son,

I suppose that before we get too involved with the anima, important as it is for a man, we should look at the woman's counterpart: the animus. This is the little man living within the woman. Actually, sometimes it is more like a group of men. The animus is the masculine element in the feminine psyche. It does not do the same things for a woman that the anima does for a man, although it is her link with the unconscious also. Some theorize that the main function of the animus is to "fertilize" the anima for a man. It is the animus that "says" the right thing at the right time that inspires the outer man to do greater things. The animus is often collective in nature. In dream figures it is sometimes revealed as a group of men, not always just one alone.

The animus empowers a woman with opinions--strong, common opinions which she herself may have never thought out or may never question. It is more like a conscience telling her what to do and say in platitudes, sometimes much to the irritation of the outer men around her. The animus and anima are autonomous complexes that ideally should be integrated into the total personality to become a function as a go-between from the conscious to the unconscious. As long as they remain unknown, hidden, or undeveloped, they cannot fulfill their proper role and continue to act like separate personalities and get projected. This integration of the anima and animus into the psychic structure, which helps make the individual whole or complete, is an idealistic state; it is never totally achieved, but the perfect woman is a long ways ahead of all other women in having the animus under control. That is, she is on her way to integrating it into her psyche and understands it and how it functions and how to relate to outer men where such will be encountered. She is then able to avoid an anima/animus exchange which so frequently happens when a man and woman, ignorant of these inner components, have at it in conflict.

The animus plays up to the anima and vice versa, but when the outer man and woman are at odds, they sometimes do not realize that the argument or fight is taking place on an inner level. The anima is possessing the man and the animus is possessing the woman and all hell breaks loose and no semblance of rationality prevails. Both are going at each other with no feeling, just emotion, as the possession incapacitates feeling. That is when lots of regretful things are said and no one knows why later on. The animus is usually the aggressor and attacks first, it being the masculine element. The

problem the woman has then is in learning to think first before she wields the stick. A woman may have tremendous destructive power when the animus is unleashed or has possession of her. She must learn to respect this power and use it only as a last resort, not her first line of defense. Mostly, this destruction comes from verbal attacks that devastate the man. The anima has the same kind of verbal destructive power and it is most often in a marriage where these "foes" battle it out no holds barred.

You do not deal with the inner woman the same way you deal with an outer woman. This is an unforgivable rule. But how do you deal with an outer woman when she tries to rattle your cage or make you lose your cool either by wrath or seduction or flirting? There are four things that can be done: 1) Become a little boy, as if you were still a child in the presence of your mother, powerless before her wrath. However, if you are seduced, this is not too practical because she will be insulted if you do not treat her like a woman. So becoming childlike and taking refuge in the mother-complex is not recommended. 2) Ignore her. This is also a form of running away; however, if she is determined and persistent, then you will have to eventually deal with her in some other fashion. 3) Marry her. Form an adult relationship with all its implications of home and family. 4) Call her bluff. She will then be forced to either meet the challenge or back down. If she is spirited and chooses to meet the challenge, you will have to deal with her as a man and will, hopefully, establish a fulfilling adult relationship. If she backs down, she is the one who runs away and becomes a little girl in the presence of the inaccessible male. The only ineffective way of dealing with a woman is number one: never react as a child and run home to mother (psychologically) or all is lost since she will lose respect for you. This is all fine in theory, but in practice a man is most apt to take refuge in the mother-complex as it is a man's most predominate complex.

How do you handle flirting? If you know what you are doing and are confident that you know yourself, you can play along. Some women only tease men and never go beyond that point. However, it could end up in a situation where you would have to deal with it in one of the four previously mentioned ways. My advice would be to keep on an even keel by ignoring her at first. This may stop it at that point. If it does not, and she is persistent, turn around and hold your ground while you call her bluff, but do not become like a child and do not let your anima possess you.

Love,   Father

December 1, 1953

Dearest Son,

How does the anima make herself known? I can only rely on my own experience. Actually, I did not discover her, she rattled my cage until I came to my senses and listened to her. It all started one summer evening many years ago (when I was about your age) while I was attending a musical theatre production. For some reason I had tickets to attend on two successive nights. The first night I watched the show with no special significance or feeling about it. I did remember, though, that there was one particular dancer in the show who caught my attention. She wore a skimpy costume and was, I thought, strikingly attractive. (It must be pointed out here that all this transpired before I ever heard of the word "anima" or "projection" or "complex." I was ignorant, unknowing as to the forces at work inside of me.)

As I said before, I ended up attending the show again the next night. Since I had already seen it once, I could devote my full attention to the dancer I saw the previous night. So during the entire performance, I watched her like a hawk, observing her every move. I studied her physical characteristics, her size, shape, coloring, etc. It was as though I had her under a microscope. Then somewhere towards the end of the show, it dawned on me. She was, without a doubt, the most beautiful woman I had ever seen up to that time. I figured that must have been the reason I became so engrossed with her in the first place and could not understand why it took so long for me to realize it. When the show ended, I was feeling sad because I felt that I had just discovered the most beautiful woman in the world and now I would probably never see her again. After the second show, I was tormented. Here I had just been given a glimpse of heaven and it was all too short, disappearing with the final curtain. For days I was miserable. I could not eat, I could not sleep, I could barely function at work. I was obsessed by that woman. I imagined all sorts of things about her and gave her attributes she probably did not have. I was in a terrible state. I was madly in love with this woman whom I did not know and never met.

I was all wrapped up in my lovely fantasy and could not be reasoned with. I knew I was obsessed, but I did not know why. I could not shake that woman out of my mind for the harder I tried the more miserable I became. After three weeks of the hellishness--but it was somewhat pleasant to be so tormented by love--I became even more obsessed. In an effort to resolve this

spell, I started to write my first novel. This, I felt, would be a way of dealing with it. Rather than act out any solution, I chose to put it on paper as a symbolic resolution of my problem. It was a form of confession that would ease the pain in my soul. I started writing the book and instead of things improving, they got worse. On top of the obsession with my imaginary love object, I became obsessed with the book. I could not stop writing. I wrote until midnight and then got up at 3:00 a.m. and kept writing until I left for work and then spent most of my working day writing. Needless to say, this lasted exactly eight days. Then I was finished. My first novel and my second obsession were then put to rest. Several days after I completed the novel, a friend gave me a book to read. I stayed up almost all night trying to finish it, but could not. I got up early the next morning to finish the last few pages and then set it down. A strange feeling came over me. I remember going outside to watch the sunrise and reflect on what I had read. It took a few minutes to sink in. I went back inside and again felt very sad, but this time, as the time I watched the final curtain in that second show, I knew the spell was broken. No longer would I be obsessed. I still thought about that woman, but I could now get my life back onto track again.

My education about the anima began. I had just received a brief taste of her powers. I was fortunate, though, in that I channeled my energy into writing, rather than acting it out. It was four months after the time I first saw that dancer that I first started communicating with my anima. My favorite anima image is the Princess image and the part the dancer played in the show was that of a princess. The unconscious projection was a natural fit and I did not realize it until months later. The anima was obviously trying to make herself known. She wanted me to get to know her, so she forced herself upon me in the possession and tormented me until I was ready to give in. I was by then a willing and receptive learner.

The difference between then and now, the passage of time and the results of having a good relationship with the anima, can best be illustrated by a recent experience. About a month ago, I had a dream in which I met a very beautiful blonde who wanted to help me accomplish something. Upon waking, I taxed my imagination to see who and what the woman in the dream represented. Obviously, she was an anima image. Then it dawned on me--based on her description and the way she was dressed in the dream--she was the woman from the book I wrote when I was obsessed with the dancer. She was the main character from my first novel! I thought it was strange, but did not pursue it any further. Later that morning when I arrived at work, I

was standing waiting for the elevator when this gorgeous, tall, sexy, blonde walks up. We looked at each other momentarily. She could probably tell that I was thinking that she was beautiful and that I knew that she knew she was also. At any rate, that was as far as our encounter went. Because I instantly realized that she was the spitting image of the woman I had just dreamed about that morning: the character in my book. That realization kept me from thinking or doing anything but questioning the meaning of that encounter. Synchronicity or fate? All I had to do was ask the anima the meaning of all this. The answer was simple: I had been grappling with an idea for a new novel and had one all outlined, but was not sure I wanted to tackle it. The blonde was the cue to signal me that it was time to get started on writing another book, but not the one I had planned. When I saw her, it reminded me of the task I had at hand and the anima informed me that she would let me know when it was time to start.

But getting back to my discovery of the anima in the first place. I mentioned that the spell of the dancer was broken after I read a book about the grail myth and what I found most striking was how the myth applied to me. I was caught up in it. Now that I have come a long way psychologically since then, I can see how the grail myth does and does not apply to our day and age. Originally, it was a myth about deeds, but times have changed. We need a new myth for our times, one that deals with feelings. The grail myth does touch upon feelings in the Fisher King wound: the torment, the suffering born out of too much Logos. But that is not significant unless taken in the context of what that suffering represents. For a man, that Fisher King wound, that suffering, that pain, is only labor pains. He must give birth to his feminine nature, his anima. She must come forth into his world, his consciousness. Until she does, he will suffer just as if he were carrying around a child inside him who was long overdue. A man will never find happiness, the Grail, until he discovers his anima and establishes a satisfactory relationship with her. Once he does, the whole world opens up to him, grail castle and all. Some even theorize that the Grail itself represents femininity in that it is shaped like the womb and one enters the grail castle to find the grail experience through the vagina. But the search for the perfect woman is in vain unless it also leads to the answer of "Whom does the Grail serve?"

Love,

Father

January 3, 1954

Dear Son,

A few letters ago I talked about women in their "childing" stage. Some women never progress past this point. She has but one mission in life: to be a mother--yours, mine, the world's. Such a woman is so bound up in mothering that when her children are grown up, she will find others to mother: grandchildren, her son-in-law, her husband, the neighbor kids, anyone. She is a mother, first, last and always--a worshiper of Aphrodite from the beginning to end, with no desire or ability for anything else.

Moving on past the childing stage, we discover the next step in feminine evolution for those who reach it. A woman in her "loving" stage, if it can be called that, is different than a man in love. But let me digress for a moment first. Instead of dolls and toy guns, children need something more basic: every little girl needs a swing and every little boy needs a wheelbarrow. A wheelbarrow for a little boy is something he pushes around in front of him keeping his focus downward, which, of course, is where his genitals are.

A swing for a little girl accomplishes several things: one, it helps her get used to picking her feet up off the ground, leaving security behind; two, she needs a push to get started, to get going, mainly symbolic of when her mother pushes her off onto her own; three, she learns to swing, that is to follow her own cycles or rhythm in her life that is right for her. As she swings up ever higher in the air, she sees the world from a different angle. Up there she gets a new perspective of the world and life that men never see.

What happens when a "wheelbarrow pusher" and a "swinger" fall in love? Ideally, they will both learn something from each other. The man will learn to swing a little, but remain basically a wheelbarrow pusher and the woman will learn to push the wheelbarrow a little, but remain a swinger. That is ideal, but usually what happens is that one goes over to the other side. The woman will then become a wheelbarrow pusher also. Or the man will become a swinger. When a man becomes a swinger, he gets dizzy up there; he is out of his realm. He cannot cope with the insecurity and unnaturalness and cannot get his life back together. But mostly, the woman ends up pushing the wheelbarrow, focusing her attention downward, rather than up over the garden wall. She will lose her unique perspective. However a paradox develops.

Even though many women end up pushing a wheelbarrow after they fall in love, men usually defer to women. The man ends up playing her game. Women have established the rules of courtship and mating and the man usually ends up "toeing the line." He has been sold a bill of goods and most of his life he will pay for it. She may help push wheelbarrows, but that is not women's work. It is man's work and, unfortunately, most men never end up doing men's work. They end up doing work that is feminine in nature. That is, they are not creative in their work. Very few men plant things, write things, paint things, build things, that is do things that are truly creative either materially or in expression. A woman's work is in gathering, spinning, weaving and sorting. And too many men are engaged in such types of occupations. A man takes his wheelbarrow and tries to organize, rush, push, etc. Woman, doing women's work which is in tune with her nature, is patient. A man could be patient also it he were to let his anima guide him, but she hates wheelbarrows and will have no part in pushing them.

Love,

Father

January 18, 1954

Dearest Son,

There are two things a woman needs: one is a mystery or secret, the other is to be elusive. A woman's greatest mystery is her ability to have children and she instinctively knows that this is her secret alone; no man can comprehend it. Her elusiveness is her way of escaping. I mentioned earlier about never cornering a woman. It bears repeating, viewing it from a different angle. If you corner a woman and she chooses to fight, she will always win. Or she will run away, just disappear, escape. Or she will become depressed, but if she does become depressed, she runs the risk of losing her mystery. But how can she regain her mystery? Very carefully. The fairytale Sleeping Beauty illustrates it perfectly.

A woman's work consists of weaving, gathering, sorting and spinning. In our story, the princess pricks her finger while spinning and falls asleep for 100 years. What this tells us is that a woman can get depressed doing any one of her feminine tasks and her escape is a deep sleep. The worst thing one can do at this point, in an effort to awaken her, is to remind her to go back to her task. The best thing to do, and the story follows suit, is to have her recapture her mystery, her beauty. It is her beauty that is asleep and must be awakened. You cannot awaken her sexually or it will fail. You wake her with beauty--a kiss--but by then she has lost her youthful innocence and has matured as represented by the passage of 100 years.

Carl Jung himself once made a statement something to the effect that man has reached his level of consciousness and cannot continue on until woman catches up. Or at least that is the gist of it. I think that they have caught up, that they are now standing eye to eye with man and that in the future it will be woman that takes the lead in moving towards more consciousness. At worst, what this may bring about is a reverting back to nature and a matriarchal society where the hand that rocks the cradle rules the world. And the price for this "peace on earth" will be that man the explorer, the developer, the creator, may be stifled--both from outside and within. But if the ideal comes to pass, woman will take the lead with man saying, "Go ahead, but we will be right behind you every step of the way." Then, possibly, Humanity will rise to the heights it never dared imagine. But will it not be through the efforts and struggle of the perfect woman? As she becomes legion, will it not be she who leads us on the next important step,

the first step? Will she not be the trailblazer who guides man to his ultimate
destiny?

   Love,

      Father

January 28, 1954

My Dear Son,

Is it possible for a man to withhold projections? That is, to keep from projecting his own unconscious femininity onto an outer woman who carries the image for him, to be the living substitute for the unknown feminine part of his own soul? That is a good question. According to Jung, once the anima is recognized and understood and integrated into the personality as a function, the keeper of the gate at the threshold of the unconscious, she no longer acts as an autonomous complex. I personally would not want to give her up. She has a useful purpose on both sides of the inner world and I would definitely miss my companion, my sometimes only friend, counselor and lover. I like having her play tricks, force me to do weird things, warn me of dangers, give me insight, act as a giver of all Wisdom, bestower of Beauty, signaler of Truth. She is the source of all Love, creativity, enthusiasm, entertainer extra ordinaire, closest confidante and inner wife. She can be mother, or guardian angel with a flaming sword. She can also be a real bitch.

But can I keep from projecting her? Yes and no. If I ask her not to let me project anything, she will accommodate me. Then I am consciously aware of myself, my anima, the multitude of images, and the types of women who can best hold my projections. But it takes conscious effort. Yet, the next minute I can let my guard down, be overtired, forgetful or feeling smug and a woman can walk into the room and attract my projection like a magnet. It is my fault, although the woman may or may not be innocent. She could be innocent and ignorant of the fact that she is a natural anima carrier and has been victimized by me, or she can be very conscious and conniving about it, knowing full well her special inclination and my weakness and attempt to exploit the situation. So it is a combination of events, or synchronicity, that makes for a projection: my unconscious acting on its own, as a natural function, and the predisposition of the woman. She must be a vessel who can hold my projection.

This same type of interaction can be applied to finding the perfect woman. The circumstances must be right. Both the man and the woman must be at a certain place in their lives at the same point in time. This confluence of factors, or synchronicity again, may or may not be realized by either, but what transpires is a feeling that both are perfect for each other and that, in and of themselves, they are both perfect, not just plain "right" for each other. But

this is only at a point in time. Given the passage of time and the continuing development of both, or lack of it, they will no longer be the same. And that change is what could very well make them totally imperfect for each other and in each other's eyes. Had they joined forces at that perfect moment and been able to have grown along the same path, they may have been able to find a perfect life together. But by not, the stars will never appear the same in the heavens and the chance is lost forever.

But what if? What if the perfect woman appears on the scene and then through one's stupidity or fate, vanishes and nothing can bring either back into their perfection together? Hopefully, another woman may come along and you will have learned your lesson the first time. But if not, keep hoping and searching, not becoming bitter or angry. Like a rainbow, if the conditions are right and you are in the right place at the right time, you will see another, but do not try too hard to find the end of it. Likewise, do not try too hard to find the perfect woman or she will elude you. You will be too preoccupied with finding her and not be attuned to the conditions, or confluences inside, that make it all possible.

Love,

Father

February 9, 1954

Dear Son,

Too oft we fall in love with the image of our soul borne by another. Forsooth we love the statue of ourselves. How many types of love there are, and how much they are abused by projections. The woman also projects her animus onto a man much the same way a man projects his anima onto a woman. The projections are similar, though subtly different, but the fact that they are projecting their own unconscious opposite nature upon another real person is the same. When both a man and a woman project onto each other, mutually, it can be called being in love. The projections, while just taking aim, or trying to be pinned onto each other, is called falling in love. At that point the projections are being tested to see if they fit or can be carried by the other. It is as if the man were trying on the woman's animus like a new suit of clothes and the woman trying on the man's anima like a new dress. After primping and preening and adjusting here and there, if the image clings, they declare that they are in love. The "falling in" part took very little time and they were not aware of the subtle dressing that was taking place. But what was put on by each was a costume, a disguise. Neither really saw the other as a real person in their own right, but only in how they fit into the costume, the wearing of the projection. Then the woman becomes the dearest, sweetest, sexiest angel in the world because she carries the projection of the man's anima perfectly. She could be a domineering bitch, but to the man that is only her strength of character. Or she could be any type of maladjusted person one could think of, but because she carries the image, the man will rationalize away all faults that are pointed out to him. He is not really in love either, but in love with his idea of being in love. The object does not matter. He has idealized his beloved beyond the rational and as long as he sees her wearing the perfect anima costume, she is perfect. But all he sees is the projection, not the real woman wearing it. Would that he could be so wise as to undress her mentally to see the real person stripped of his idealization. But, alas, it is all unconscious.

And the woman is projecting in the same fashion. And as they profess their undying love for each other, they find they are sexually compatible. So it further goes to prove that they are ideally suited for each other and should get married. And they do. And after the "I do's" are said and done, they go off on their honeymoon. And with the courtship and wedding beyond them, they can settle down and be themselves. But after a few anima/animus

exchanges, the costumes get tattered and torn and the real individual begins to show through. This may happen early or take many years, but when the costumes have all been removed and they realize that each is different than the idealization and projection led them to believe, the honeymoon is said to be over. Now they are just two, plain, less than perfect adults who must try to put together a relationship based on each other's reality. This may succeed or fail. The shock of realizing that "you're not the woman I thought I married" may be too great to allow a basis for a realistic mature relationship. Feeling deceived or deluded, either one or both may decide to call it quits. But...the next time around the same thing happens because the projecting and idealizing are all on an unconscious level. So they both end up back at the costume store again to shop for a summer wardrobe. If both or one of them has realized the process that swept them off their feet in the first place and learned something about themselves and their opposite nature, then there is some hope that mistakes in the future can be minimized.

The anima, as reflected by an infinite number of feminine images, is constantly in a state of flux. You cannot always know at any point which image is present. If you were "anima poor," you might have only one or two images such as Mother or Prostitute. But when highly developed or "anima rich," you can have countless images coming and going all day and night. Again, dream images are one good way to discover the different images present in the unconscious. Another way is to ask what image is present through active imagination. Sometimes fantasies give a clue. But if you have a good relationship with her, you can ask that a certain image come forth. She may not always be accommodating, but most of the time she will. For example, there are many times that I know I have to relate to a particular woman. I want to hit it off right with her, so I ask the anima if she will help me relate to that woman through the Wife image. (Although it is best to let the anima choose how best to relate and pick the proper image, for the Wife image may not be the appropriate image at that time.) The anima is much more intuitive and can quickly, through trial and error, come up with the best image to relate through under the given circumstances. To a degree, she is very useful and gives one an advantage over others who have little knowledge of their unconscious make-up, but such an advantage is the outcome of a close relationship with the anima.

Let's look at how having a good relationship with the anima and being able to control, or withhold, projections helps you with love. By not projecting, you can see the other person in their own right, with all their

faults, phobias, bad moods, bad habits, etc. You can see the real person and, by not having them carry around or being burdened with your projection, you can relate in fact, not fantasy or idealization.

So, whenever I hear someone say, "We're in love" or "I've just fallen in love," I think of the myriad projections taking place. But that feeling, that glorious roller-coaster, merry-go-round, butterflies-in-the-stomach feeling--it is the greatest of all feeling--the ultimate and I would not want to disillusion you or make it lose any of its magic. Yet how much grander it could be if you really were loving someone, a real person, not an illusion. You can love the perfect woman, but you will never see her reality if you project or idealize. And she will see right through the projections and refuse to wear the costume. She wants love, not the idea of love that is bound up in a projection. Your projections will drive the perfect woman away.

Love,

Father

February 24, 1954

My Dear Son,

Do you remember earlier when I briefly touched upon a woman's loving stage in my discussion of wheelbarrows and swings? Initially her "loving" stage starts out with tender love and many women never get beyond that tender love stage. Until approximately the time she reaches her mid-thirties, a woman is, if in a loving frame of mind, at a tender love stage. Many women never develop beyond this point because they are deterred by a husband and children, mostly children. Her consciousness evolves around her family and does not seek to go past that realm. Or if she is drawn to its calling, she represses it because of her duty or obligation to her family. If she does enter this higher plateau, it is because of her swinging experience and she is able to view herself and the world with a different perspective. But more importantly she must be willing to risk. Here is where many women turn back, for she must be willing to risk everything.

To be able to risk it all is a condition many women cannot accept. Some "turn back" by repressing, for they fear losing control, of becoming dizzy or disoriented, as they soar over the garden wall on their swing. But when a woman does let go and risk it all, it means her home, children, everything. She has freed herself and is no longer in love with a man, but is in love. At this point we can use the term being in love. I did not mean "being in love" as in "falling in love" as differentiated by loving someone and projecting. She is not in love with love, but is "a being" in love--her whole existence is bound up in her loving nature. The problem some women encounter at this phase is that they end up getting attached to a man who is not worthy of them: a Don Juan or ne'er-do-well. However, if she is of supreme character and does not fall for the wrong type, she can become discriminating as to whom she will let inside her "in love" experience. Usually it will be a man of resource.

By a man of resource I do not mean one who is able to support her or lavish her in wealth, but one who has the resources she needs and is able to relate to her because of his maturity and understanding. Unfortunately, there are as few men of resource as there are women in this loving stage. For both conditions are born out of an expanding consciousness that few people are willing to undertake. That leads to her next problem. Since there are so few men able to relate to her, or bring the necessary resources into a relationship,

she may become disappointed and disillusioned. But really it is a disappointment with herself and she unconsciously sets out to destroy men because she has lost her "being" in love. Others may take a more passive approach and just end up suffering because they have entered their mystery of being in love and have no place to go with it. Do you somehow get the impression that to discover the perfect woman you must encounter her at this stage in her development? Her whole being is in love and she is seeking a man who is her equal. It is a rare man who can fulfill her need because most men do not understand what is going on inside her. Her nature is different and it is filled with love. Men do not have a parallel and must, therefore, be very sensitive and wise to relate to them at this point. It is only after many years, much soul searching and heeding the call of her inner dictates that a woman arrives at her loving stage. It is also after much suffering and bidding tender love adieu that she is able to take that step towards paradise.

Love,

Father

March 10, 1954

Dear Son,

How should you approach an outer woman? Obviously, the approach is important because unless you can meet her and get to know her, you will never discover her true being and may thereby overlook, or be oblivious to, what could be a perfect woman. Never approach a woman through the thinking function as it will always fail. For a man, the thinking function is the logical or masculine approach. In this realm of Logos, man is on his own ground and no woman, or very few, would dare to relate on foreign territory. Hers is a world of Eros, or relationship, that transcends logic. A woman is at home with feelings, although she holds no monopoly on them. To say that feeling is predominately woman's is a generality and not a universal truth. So the question is: If you should not approach a woman through the thinking function, should you approach her through the feeling function?

Everyone assumes that if feeling is a woman's realm, then that is the best approach, to meet her on her own ground. Yes and no. Relating to her through the feeling function may prove successful for a while, but that, too, will eventually fail. For a man, sometimes, by having a dominant thinking function, will be totally "out of water" using this approach. As I have said before, I have that problem so I know how well it can fail. Mostly because when a man gets bound up in feeling, he is subject to contamination by his mother-complex or his anima. Both of these can appear to be feelings and interfere, but are not true feelings. They are false and in time a woman will discover it. She has a keen sense for ferreting out false feeling, as it is her nature.

What then is the successful way to approach her? Through the anima! But not as a projection or possession. First you must tell the anima that you want to relate through her and not to project anything. Then you must trust her to pick the right image to relate through. This is done by trial and error through her intuition. She zeroes in on an image, tries it, and if it does not fit, quickly adopts another one. This is all done very quickly and without conscious knowledge as to how it is being done, because no one really understands how this works. The mechanics of relating through the anima cannot be broken down and put under a psychic microscope. Surprisingly, it is possible that more than one image may fit. Women like continuity, but are very changeable. So you must keep up the continuity of relating only

through the anima and be adaptable to the image as the outer woman changes. But certain cautions are in order: make sure the anima image is appropriate. Always relate to your wife through the Wife image, although you can relate to other women through that image also. But never relate to your wife through the Prostitute image, nor to any other woman except a prostitute. Sometimes, on rare occasions, no image seems to fit; the woman is a vamp who is only out to rattle your cage. The best suggestion is no image at all. Avoid her if at all possible for who knows what her game is. She could be just a plain frustrated woman, psychotic, or turned sour in her loving stage and out to destroy men.

If you encounter such a woman--run! Run away physically, if possible. If not, take refuge in the mother-complex. If you can escape for a breathing spell, consult the anima as to what course of action is best. If she advises further avoidance, take heed; however, if she has intuited a weak spot that can be attacked to render such a woman ineffective or drive her away in search of easier prey, it may be possible to do so. But do not engage in an anima/animus exchange with her. Dazzle her with fancy words and deft logic--paradoxical logic would be an item to carry in your bag of tricks. Methodically play up to her animus, but not with your anima. Use knowledge about the animus to use against her. How cruel and cutting you need to be only you can determine, but use it only in self-defense and only as much as is necessary. But you must be conscious of what you are doing and not let her get an advantage. If the battle looks like it is going in her favor, retreat. Do not get caught behind enemy lines. This does go counter to what I said earlier about how to deal with a woman when she tries to make you lose your cool through wrath or seduction or flirting. That was in the context of a normal woman using normal wiles. It is all part of a friendly game, a sane one. What we have here is a dangerous game. She just may not have all her oars in the water and, if that is the case, sail clear or she will sink your ship. This, I know, is in direct contrast to the perfect woman. Our goal is to find her, but on such a journey you may encounter Medusa. It is as important to know what is NOT the perfect woman as it is to know what is. Lilith lurks everywhere.

Love,

Father

March 23, 1954

Dearest Son,

I have already told you about projections and how the different anima images can be projected. Even though there are an infinite number of images, the dialogue between the anima and animus reveals four basic patterns. All images have one thing in common: femininity; but from there, the nuances, or divisions which seem to apply to the "soul-classifications," fall into four categories. All these four types of "soul patterns" are present in every individual man, but only one of them is dominant. Bound up in the projection of the anima, therefore, is not only an image but also this unconscious attitude. The man, when projecting the anima image is also dealing with his unconscious attitude or predisposition.

The four anima patterns for the man are: creativity (spirit), relations, intuition, and Sophia (earthy wisdom). The corresponding patterns for the woman are those of power, deeds, words, and logic. When one of these attitudes is projected along with the anima image, the animus responds in kind with its own corollary: the animus responds to creativity with power, to relations with deed, to intuition with words, and to Sophia with logic. The conscious side of this unconscious attitude projection can best be explained by saying that men of power look for spirit in a woman; men of deeds look for affection or relationship in a woman; men of words look for intuition in a woman; and men of logic look for earthy wisdom in a woman.

Men will try to seek out their psychic opposite in a woman and the animus will respond, but women do not necessarily look for their psychic opposite in a man. It is the man who is trying to find his soul in a woman; it is femininity that a man is searching for, even though it does exist within himself, but he is blind to it. Once he discovers his anima, his inner woman, he has his soul and no longer has to search for it in outer woman by projecting his anima. He can stop projecting his inner woman, develop a relationship with her, and that enables him to have a conscious, meaningful relationship with outer women devoid of idealizations.

Love,

Father

April 12, 1954

Dear Son,

Alas, I have the fear that if I should ever encounter a perfect woman she will be searching for the perfect man and our orbits will never coincide. Somehow I feel that she may be too elusive to describe. Maybe too perfect to even begin to put into words. So radiant, so dazzling that if she were to walk up to me, I would be so overcome and enchanted that my powers of speech would cease to function and my mind would fail to comprehend all that it could not elucidate anyway. Hence, the futility of it all, for I would probably be so naive that I would forget to reach out and touch her to see if she were real, rather than a figment of my imagination. But my search for her will not be in vain.

I have only attempted to describe her, to expose her, to find her. And there is no failure in an attempt; failure comes with the abandoning of all possible attempts. My success lies in motion--movement towards my goal. I fail the moment I stop, be it to rest or lie down in defeat. Will she let me rest? Will she call me like the Siren, luring me on with the promise of eternal bliss? To a true adventurer, a quest is an obsession that will never cease until realized. Some men search for sunken treasure, others for the answers held in outer space. I am doomed to carry on the quest for the perfect woman, be she discoverable like the source of the Nile or as elusive as Atlantis. Where is she now? Besides daring me to continue on, she is always just around the next corner. She drags me across long stretches of imagination and through the depths of the unconscious to the very gates of hell. Yet again to soar into the heavens to glimpse for a fleeting moment the wonders of paradise and then to set me gently down at my desk and bid me, "Write, search, create." But never does she promise me "find." How often have I trudged through the promised land, unaware, unable to stop, to recognize it, to savor it. My soul has feet that are a slave to motion, so off again I go... to the land of windmills.

Love,

Father

April 26, 1954

My Dear Son,

The temptation is to clutter your mind and imagination with too many details. The quest for the perfect woman does not need to be detracted from by drawing on too many symbols or analogies. But still the temptation is strong to burden you with such related topics as the shadow, active imagination, dream interpretation, complexes, etc. To bring it all in would cloud the issue and over-tax your imagination. I almost feel, though, that by avoiding such topics and not discussing them, I am shirking a responsibility, although it is your responsibility to have knowledge in these areas because they are the very essentials of life.

Any child, when asked to draw a picture of his hand, will give a good account by sketching something that resembles a hand with five fingers. He has an awareness of himself and that his hand is a physical part of him. He can communicate that awareness by drawing a picture. As an adult, such a person should have extended his awareness of himself to know how he functions consciously and what some of his unconscious elements are. Such simple things as knowing if you are introverted or extraverted should be basic knowledge.

If I can impart one thing, forgetting all the others, it is that unless you know what is going on inside, you will never be able to relate to anyone else through your true self. It will be through anima projections, shadow and mother-complexes, anima feelings, possessions, etc. You will never have a real face to present to another human being. And if you do not know the score about yourself or what face others see, how can you be sure what they are really like. Then everyone you encounter will be a stranger, but only because you are a stranger to yourself. Even disregarding the fact that if everyone were fortunate to become totally integrated personalities, there would still be a wall between people because no one else can understand what is at your core. You cannot describe your Self to someone else and must remain, of necessity, a mystery to others, but NOT to yourself. No one will ever be able to read your thoughts, correctly interpret your motives, understand your feelings, experience your sensations, etc. It is all individual. But if you know yourself, you can have some degree of measure as to how others may be functioning or dysfunctioning. You will see how you tick and the similarities--the collective unconscious we all share--which makes

describing a man the same as Man. Then knowing what makes women function as they do will help you understand your sister, mother, wife, co-workers, lover, or whatever woman you meet. The basics will be the same. So that when you do meet the perfect woman....

What I have just tried to convey in the preceding was aptly put in two words many, many centuries ago by the Greeks. For over 30 years those two words have inspired me. But finally I am beginning to understand what they mean: KNOW THYSELF. All the secrets of the universe are contained in those two words. If you know yourself, when something unusual happens, or some new inner experience is felt, it will not throw you. You can give all to that moment and then reflect later upon its meaning, knowing that it was a part of you and that it was meant to happen, that the conditions were right and you met the challenge. It is in this way that we grow and evolve toward wholeness. It is also the path followed by the perfect woman.

Love,

    Father

May 13, 1954

Dear Son,

I may have told you before that the anima has some negative traits. One of these is jealousy. She can become jealous of outer woman, feeling that the outer woman will displace her, but the paradox lies in the fact that the outer woman does displace her as the guiding principle in a man's life when he is ignorant of her and projects her onto outer woman who then acts as the anima for him. Many times she will try to drive a wedge between a man and his wife or lover. This she has the power to do and how many divorces are the result of this are unknown. Either by the animosity she creates or the luring away effect she has on a man by transferring the anima image to another woman to carry, she can cause a man to end up wherever she wants him. However, she could be only trying to create a conflict that will force the man to grow psychologically.

Since the anima empowers a man with images of love and desire, she is the one who says to love this one or that one, but shouldn't be the feeling itself. To that degree, then, the feeling function is a tool of the anima, it is like a control panel she operates. If you have a poor relationship with her, that is, know little or nothing about her, she will control that feeling panel at her will. If you have a good relationship with the anima, your feeling function is then ego oriented, although she continues to have access to it. You can allow her to use it, but she will not have exclusive control. It can be shared. Many feelings a man has are all anima-inspired. She can, as I said before, even act as a substitute for the feeling function itself.

The images she offers provide channels for feelings. She brings you the feelings; the feeling function handles them. You can ask her to bring only good feelings, but what she brings are neither bad nor good. The feelings are really neutral that she brings. The thinking function assigns meaning; the feeling function determines value. After all, feelings are only emotions in the context of meaning and value. The most prevalent context for meaningful emotions to express themselves through is love. But by being feminine herself and bringing feelings, it is only natural that she is motivated by feeling, not thinking. You can communicate and reason with her, but not through the use of logic necessarily. To a degree, she can be reasoned with, but mostly through emotional appeals and feeling. She must be dealt with on a feeling level. What she says is always the truth (if you have a good

relationship), but remember that inner truths are not necessarily the same as outer truths. Also, what she informs is always accurate and her opinions and observations and insights are uncanny. So, what she thinks, says and feels you can trust, if you have a good relationship with her, but what she does is another matter.

What can she do? Just about anything she wants. And if you have no knowledge of her, she may drive you to drink or some other self-destructive habit. But how can she have such destructive powers? Will not she be destroying herself, too? No. As an unconscious phenomenon, her roots are in the collective unconscious and the unconscious knows no death, only change. How then can she have such great power?

By possessing you. By overpowering your ego to be the driving force in both the conscious and unconscious. An anima possession normally causes you to lose your ability to feel and when strong enough, even to think. Normally, under a possession you are in a mood that you do not understand nor have any control over. At its worst, you can be thought to be suffering from amnesia or possessed by a demon. You are not really any of the above. What you are, in fact, is a pseudo-woman. You have no masculine qualities about you save your physical body and that may cease to function as a man's also. If she chooses, she may cut off the sex urge and make you impotent.

Mostly, though, she does not get that extreme; she can allow you to have a normal sex life. But how normal is it? Without knowing her, you cannot have a real relationship with an outer woman (only as a carrier of your anima) and that means that sex may not be really fulfilling. In this sense, sex remains purely physical as the spiritual aspect is missing because sex ought to mean the joining of two souls. How can you merge with a woman's soul when your own "soul" is projected out of yourself onto an outer woman?

The anima can possess you in other subtle ways that you are unaware of. Drinking is one area that is anima territory. Some men think it is manly to be able to drink a lot. Some do drink excessively, but the ensuing hangover is the anima laughing at him for the trick she played. In its worst form, such a possession may lead to alcoholism. Some view it as a disease, a physical addiction, a psychological problem, but in a man it may very well be an anima possession of the worst kind. The end result is destruction. But how does this come about? If you have a bad relationship with her or none at all, she may drive you to drink. She lures you on, seducing you with the grand

and glorious heights to which you rise as you lose your inhibitions. This freeing of repressed feeling, for some men, is the only feeling they experience and they value it highly. So it becomes easier and easier to be lured into something that offers a reward. The payoff is the experiencing of feeling--be it good or bad--and is the only time that some men have any relationship with their inner self. But the euphoria is addictive and becomes a bad habit, but is still an anima trick.

But how can such a bad habit be broken? By getting to know her, by establishing a good relationship and asking her to help. But it takes faith, determination and trust. It also requires a humbleness to be willing to submit to her voice, something previously unknown and ignored. She will have her say. You will listen...or else....

I know this all sounds a little dire. The majority of men never get that bad off. Some are fortunate enough to escape any destructive-like possessions. But sometimes possessions are desirable. If you have knowledge of her and understand her, she can and should possess you to enable you to create. She is the creative spirit and is necessary if creation is to take place. Creation is a feminine function: motherhood, mother earth, etc., although some will argue that the masculine must be present also. The two opposites uniting are necessary. Viewed from that point then, it is the feminine nature in the masculine that enables creation. Art, music, poetry, etc., are all creative and stems from the anima in a man. Usually it is the anima in the form of a possession. But you do not always have to have knowledge of the anima to be able to create. That is obvious in some creative people when they run into a mental block or just seem to turn unproductive. It is the anima withholding her energy, or most likely channeling it off somewhere else in some other type of possession.

The other area where an anima possession is necessary is in loving. This kind of possession is obviously constructive and is the outcome of a good relationship. Does this mean that if you have no understanding of your anima you cannot love? Not necessarily. But the love will not have real "soul" in it because, again, it is in the form of a projection. Then we have the old "falling" in love or being in love that precludes real loving.

I have already mentioned creativity and love as two activities where an anima possession is desirable. Sometimes anima feelings may be useful, but that is not the same as a possession. Relating through the anima is definitely

not a possession. Do not try to relate through a possession. Relating to a woman without the ability to feel or think properly is a disaster.

But is creative thinking an area where the anima should have free rein? My experience says yes. The creative aspect calls for it. Even if thinking is not her realm, she is most valuable and helpful as a partner. As an inner wife, she can use her superior intuition to shed a different light on certain aspects you may have never considered. Her diffused awareness helps you to see the bigger picture and even her feelings can connect you to certain mental relationships that would have been impossible without her presence. Whenever I do anything creative I ask her to be present, to join in. It has its advantages. But you must be able to look at her contribution with a critical eye. For example, I was once contemplating the meaning of a verse in the Bible: "Lest ye become like little children, ye shall never enter the kingdom of Heaven." My early interpretation based on Sunday school was that only children or old people who have become senile will ever get into Heaven. Later it expanded from philosophical reading to mean that only if you accept religion on the level of a gullible child will you get in, that a child believes without question and has faith in things that do not have to be proven.

Asking the anima to help interpret this on a psychological level, it takes on a whole different meaning. It is only when we become like children who, when very young, do not distinguish the unconscious from the conscious will we find the kingdom of heaven within. To them there is no division--dreams seem real, goblins exist, fantasy is as real as the world of adults. They stand at the threshold of the unconscious soon getting ready to leave it for the world of the conscious. But at that point in childhood, the conscious and unconscious are both working together in harmony, each having a share in the whole. Only through time does the unconscious slip back into the unknown as the child grows and is bombarded by only the conscious as he is made to conform in an adult world. To go back as a child means to reunite the unconscious part of the being with the conscious; to be able to integrate both worlds in a unique whole within oneself once again. The heaven within is achieved by the uniting of opposites within the realm of the conscious and unconscious. Paradise lost is growing up for a child. Paradise regained is rediscovering the unconscious as an adult and reuniting both worlds that once existed only briefly in childhood. You must be humble enough to go back home again and submit yourself to the strange world of the unconscious wherein truly live the dragons, the myths, the fairytales. These all were real for the child and are even more real in the individuated adult who allows it

to come alive again inside. This view inward again through child's eyes
allows you to see the collective unconscious and the vastness of the universe
and the heaven that is always present in everyone of us--choose we to seek
it.

Love,

Father

May 25, 1954

Dearest Son,

We are concerned mainly with the feminine, but the anima's counterpart must be considered because the animus does exert an influence on the woman and enters into relationships between men and women. We must continue to view it from every possible angle. First, the animus is the inner man of a woman, just as I've said before. A woman's inner husband, if you will, just like the anima is a man's inner wife. It, too, can be projected and usually is. The animus also has many different images. These are about the only similarities between the animus and the anima. Some typical animus figures may be a grandfather, an ancient hero, an old professor, a movie star, a singer, etc. Many times, especially in dreams, animus figures appear in groups. The number of figures in the group may be significant. Numbers in dreams are relevant to inner psychic processes and I would venture a guess that the number of the group for most women would be 2, 3, or more, but seldom 4. Three would probably be most common as it signifies a dynamic state, that of struggling, growing, evolving, an inner tension. Four would signify unity or wholeness that is the aim of an integrated Self. I suspect that the perfect woman would be accustomed to the number four, but more likely to the number one, for one would be symbolic of the integrated Self or the animus as the go-between from the conscious to the unconscious. As a function, rather than an autonomous complex, he loses his plurality.

The average woman's animus will have both a bad side and a good side, or one figure will represent the dark side of her personality while another figure will represent the positive side. It is enough to point out this helpful and disruptive aspect of the animus. What does the animus do? Like the anima, he is the source of creativity. The animus, as I mentioned once before, gives a woman an opinionated attitude. The other real beneficial aspect of the animus is that he helps illuminate that part of her psyche that is not clear to her. He helps her distinguish the various parts of her total being that are not always that well understood. A woman needs her animus to help her perceive details: one thing that is difficult for her and to help her concentrate, especially where her tasks are involved for her view of life and of her tasks are too broad. Unlike the anima, the animus is her link with the world of Logos. He does not bring feelings, nor does he even have any feelings. A woman has feelings and does not need the animus to supply them as in the case of a man who needs his anima to help with feelings.

Animus opinions are a disruptive aspect of the inner man and what he imparts can be found in any book of familiar quotations. Many women accept this as gospel and never question the source or validity of this animus verbiage. I was reading a book recently written by a woman. It was an affront to intelligence. The pages were rife with quotes out of context, opinions, suppositions, and self-proclaimed truths. I just shrugged it off. It was just dripping with negative animus; a classic example of how the animus irritates and alienates men with its banality.

The perfect woman knows and understands and can discern what is happening when this negative animus appears. She can communicate with her animus to have him informed of her stance, her beliefs, her feelings and thereby has a good relationship with her animus which helps her avoid that bumper-sticker mentality.

Love,

Father

June 8, 1954

Dearest Son,

    I have already presented love via "falling" and "being" in love. Love is such a vast subject. It is like a rainbow where its beauty lies in all the shades relative to each other, each particular color being a different form of love. Some describe love as a miracle, a gift from God, the basic emotion, the highest expression of human awareness. For all that love is praised as being, it is little practiced in reality. More people seek love than heaven; more products have been sold with the promise of love attached; more has been written about it, sung about it. But what is it? If it could be canned and sold in the grocery store, what price would it bring? How much would it take to satisfy you? Would you share it with your neighbor? If you had enough, would you still search for happiness? Believe it or not, all you have heard and read about love or seen in the movies is not where it is at. That is what they feed everyone because it sells. It means money in someone's pocket and the appetite is never satiated.

    You cannot buy love; you cannot search for love; you cannot force someone to love you. But...but you can attract it or set up the conditions that foster it by being loving, that is, having a loving outlook. How is this done? By allowing the anima to let it shine forth. But it cannot be done if you do not know where the source of love is--if you cannot understand what it is or how it functions. It can only be found by discovering and understanding her; it is a gift to you from the gods, her link with Eros. If you do not know her, you are doomed to "being" in love or "falling" in love, but never really "loving." Then love is nothing more than a projection, an anima-complex feeling, an idealization, not true love. It is a false love that will fade when reality creeps in to wash away the projection or when the costume wears thin. True, you have no control over love, especially in attracting it from others, but you can ally yourself with the anima so her channeling of love can flow out through you constructively. So then, to love, you can have the resources to meet another person's needs.

> Do I still love you today?
> I hope my love is like a tree,
> And everyday it grows and grows;
> And then one day
> To reach the sky;

Its roots are deep
To withstand drought;
The limbs are strong
To support all cares,
And winds of change
May bend it some,
But it won't break or fall;
It weathers well
And gives cooling shade
To all the tired who pass by;
And when its leaves
Begin to die,
It is that tree
That still stands tall.

Love,

Father

June 20, 1954

Dear Son,

    I often suspect that, after all is said and done, the perfect woman may turn out to be a divorcee. Somehow I feel that only after the first blush of tender love fades from the cheeks of our once fair flower, will the conditions become right for that inner growth so necessary if one is to find wholeness. Is that to say that marriage keeps one from becoming perfect, or that one can become perfect only after experiencing a bad marriage? The answer is a resounding NO. Marriage is not to blame. It is the lack of understanding of the unconscious forces of the anima and animus that usually ruin the marriage. That is not the institution's fault, but the ignorant individuals who embarked on a premature venture. It is unfortunate that only after such a disaster and the passing of time is it possible for many people to begin to look inside and see what part they played in making a mess out of what could have been paradise. The inner man and inner woman were not ready for marriage because they were never invited, but dragged along against their will. Had they been consulted in the first place--a condition precluded by lack of knowledge of their existence--things would have maybe been manageable. The partners could then have coped, compromised, communicated and co-existed with the help of their inner mates rather than their hindrance.

    But little do we know too soon. There should be a second marriage ceremony where the man and woman have their anima and animus joined in matrimony. Usually, though, the only time those neglected inner components have their say is in divorce court. So what happens? The woman whose nature is love and was trusting and optimistic "fell" in love and, over time, became disillusioned and disappointed. Her knight on a big white horse turned out to be an ass on a donkey and the hero image faded. The overgrown little boy she married could no longer carry her animus projection and idealism vanished. Her animus was not there to help sustain her. He was too busy foxing up the air with post-card platitudes and antagonizing the man's anima. Worse than children those inner children can be. So she ended up with an extra child--the one she married and he ended up with an extra mother, or shrew, or whatever he views her as. After the divorce, the shock and loneliness may be enough of a blow to have her start listening to her inner man and begin to grow, or she may go to an analyst who will hopefully put her back on the right track.

Sadly, I have seen many divorced women and can see why they are. Rarely, though, I have seen one or two that are beginning on their way. Hopefully they will become what can be called perfect, but not yet. Perfection is a journey and they have not logged enough miles yet.

> Lovely lady yet so young
> For whom only once was sung
> The blissful songs of married love,
> Who now casts herself a failure
> Because it was not sealed above
> Forever by a choir of angels--
> Please don't give up hope;
> Are you now a dying ember
> That one time was passion's flame,
> Destined never again to glow
> Because of one loss in love's game?
> Don't be so foolish!
> Wisdom only comes with time;
> Love must ripen like all things;
> Give yourself another chance
> To find the joy experience brings.
> So young and naive with the first one;
> Invest your being in your duty;
> Only a promise rests in the bud. . .
> It's the flower that has beauty.

I am sure everyone realizes that some women are more perfect than others--having more poise, courage, inner strength, character and wisdom than others. Maybe they are not perfect, only more fortunate; but then it would look silly to search for the fortunate woman, because "perfect" seems to have a special mystical quality about it, especially in our society where everyone is taught to strive, improve, grow, learn, get ahead. Perfection is the crowning glory, the highest achievement on earth. Surely once it is attained, even heaven is assured. But, ironically, the perfect woman is often overlooked. She wears no sign that proclaims her perfection. Even those around her sometimes miss it because she is so often misunderstood. That is a sign in itself, for how can anyone understand someone either far superior or more highly evolved. I use the word "evolved" to mean consciousness.

The perfect woman has expanded her level of consciousness far beyond

her peers. Sad, but being far above them, she is in a sense isolated, but not to mean lonely (as opposed to a woman isolated from life because of a negative animus possession). She knows where her being is centered and how that center relates to the world and that gives her a freedom no one else can comprehend. The more she becomes herself, enlarges herself, the farther she moves away from the humanity around her and moves closer to heaven, the God within. She is then able to give of herself from the essence of her being because her energy is freed from the mundane. She becomes more Godlike and that brings her closer to humanity. The paradox is that as she rises above the commonness to reach the level of perfection, she is more attuned to the commonness, but not restrained by it. She has wandered away from the crowd of women to become Woman. She is then truly in touch with the Feminine, the archetype that is synonymous with Creation and Soul. Then being a woman takes on a new meaning; it is fulfilling her destiny. She partakes of the universe and, though she is only a small part of it, she is a part that is essential and keeps it alive.

Love,

Father

July 3, 1954

Dearest Son,

All women are basically alike. They all look alike physically; they all have their own individual feminine cycles. They all have their basic feminine psychology that does not differ much from one to the next. Why, then, is it so hard for a man to understand them? Because man is born of woman. He is different from the moment of birth and his mother realizes it. Never will that boy baby be able to identify with its mother. He is raised differently. There is a special separateness that does not exist between a mother and a girl infant. The mother knows that this one belongs to the inner circle and is welcomed in. A boy is the "runt of the litter." He gets the same milk, love and care as a girl does, but he is destined from birth to remain outside the mystery. And even if he should spend a lifetime trying to fathom the feminine unknown, he will never succeed. He can know about women intellectually, understand how they function physically, even probe their psychological nature. But he is still a man and all he can really know about women is what his anima supplies--his small link with womanhood that exists within himself.

However, that small feminine component within himself is a woman, much of which he fails to understand also. If he were to set out to establish a good relationship with her, and form a bond of love and trust, she would unveil the secrets of womanhood to him far beyond what even some women know about themselves. All the time spent studying women is in vain. Just ask the anima and she will inform everything. But the ironic paradox is: how many men, when they want to understand women, bother to look for answers within their own soul.

Most men when hearing that there is a feminine component existing within them are repulsed. They view this as a sign of weakness, an inferior invasion of something that will cause them to be emotional and defile their manliness. These ignoramuses can be seen everywhere as macho supermen who equate "being a man" with sex. To be a big man, to them, means to run up a big score in bed. But these are little men who soon succumb to that little inner woman who gets sick and tired of being ignored or not being able to express herself. She becomes a woman scorned and hell is when the anima turns enemy. In its mildest form, a man just becomes moody, loses satisfaction with his work or family, feels an emptiness or looks around and

asks, "Is this all there is to life?" In its worst form, the anima may wreak havoc in his life. A man's mid-life crisis is a badge he wears on his sleeve to indicate to the world that he has no relationship with his anima–a person who truly does not Know Thyself.

Love,

Father

July 16, 1954

My Dear Son,

Lest I seem neglectful, I should mention that others, such as psychologist Toni Wolff who was a close associate of Carl Jung, have tried to further classify women beyond the four psychological types. Since the psychological categories include thinking, feeling, intuition and sensation, I will have to call these four others "personality" types.

The first is the maternal type. She has her optical nerve attached to her umbilical cord. She has a persistent and pervasive mothering outlook on life. Her world revolves around her home and family. At its worst, it is overdone and she identifies with the Great Mother, becomes the Great Mother and raises hell for those around her. I have only encountered two women who I would say fit this category, one when I was a youngster, the other as an adult.

The first, I remember her well because that is when I learned the word "bitch," was the mother of a classmate. She was overprotective, overindulgent, henpecked her husband beyond belief and her little darlings could do no wrong. I learned about her from my other friends because their mothers told them to steer clear of HER! She had the mission in life of telling all the neighborhood mothers the Right and Proper Way to Raise Your Children. But it was her brats that no one could stand. She was the negative mother, the all-devouring female who had no other interest or direction in life.

The only other woman I knew that could fit this maternal category was a woman who had not yet had any children. All she talked about was the day that she would become pregnant. When she did, that was the only subject in the world. Her vocabulary consisted of three words: babies, babies, babies. She gave morning sickness to everyone around her, even long after she delivered. Her maternal instincts have overshadowed the rest of her personality and left little else to shine through.

The next type is the companion. She is as gung-ho about relationships as the maternal type is about babies. To her, the highest value in life is represented by relationships. Here Eros has her by the throat the same as Aphrodite has the maternal type in her grasp. Fortunately or unfortunately, this type is a good anima carrier for a man and attracts it either unknowingly

or knowingly. Some women are more able to attract and carry a man's anima projection than others. These types are often misunderstood and often unaware that they themselves are the carriers of the projections. They may be unaware of their unique ability or they may recognize it and use it to the man's disadvantage. If a woman knows she can attract their images and deliberately does, she may compromise him to gain power, wealth, or whatever else she wants, knowing full well that the man is putty in her hands as long as she holds the image for him. But is it her fault for taking advantage of him, or is it his fault for projecting in the first place and getting himself into the mess? A good question.

If he is ignorant of his anima and projects it, he cannot be held liable for doing what he does not know he is doing. But if he knows his anima and then still projects, he is to blame. Or is he? What about the anima possessing him and forcing him to project as a trick which in the long run may save him from something worse? Is it a man's fault for projecting? No. The anima will always be projected to some degree. It can never be held back completely. To do so would turn her into a function--which is what she should be--but that is only a goal, a striving. If one could withhold all projections and have the anima act exclusively as a function would rob a man of a certain richness and beauty in his life. There would be no more mystery about women; there would be perfection within one's grasp.

The next personality type we want to look at is the independent type, the female counterpart of a macho-man. This type of woman feels equal to men in every respect and, deep down in the hidden recesses that are never revealed, actually feels superior to men and looks down upon them. She has her own goals in life and pursues them. At best, she will tolerate men as overgrown, egotistical children and has no real need for a man. She is not necessarily the dedicated career woman who, out of a conscious choice, decides not to get married and have a family. Hers is a choice and she may well even later regret that choice, but it was not her attitude against men that prompted her decision. She may well later on in life get married or abandon her career. Just because she is a career woman and independent financially does not mean that she fits this category. It is a matter of attitude. Likewise, some independent women who have very little use for men do get married because of the maternal instinct. You must remember that each of these four categories I am describing is in its pure state. In reality, though, a woman may fit into more than one of these and usually does. It is not unusual to find the companion type mixed with this independent type. The good carrier of

the anima may well dislike men and end up taking advantage of her special predisposition to manipulate them. The companion type could also be mixed with the maternal type. The combinations are numerous.

Again, because looks can be deceiving, it must be noted that just because a woman appears to be independent does not mean that she is and has no real need for a man. It is worth noting that a woman who is integrated and whole has an independent air about her that could be mistaken. She, then, a perfect woman, could very easily be viewed as this independent type and, by not probing deeper beneath the surface, could be overlooked as perfect. It is unfortunate that the two are so closely related on the surface. The independent woman has an attitude towards men that keeps relationships at bay. The perfect woman is truly independent, in spirit, as she is her own person and her attitude is reflected in her much broader view of life and herself--her expanded consciousness.

The last type is often called the mediator type. This type of woman helps a man get in touch with his inner nature. She serves a very useful function, almost like an external anima. She is rare and often unnoticed. Often she is unaware of this special quality much as the companion type is unaware of her anima carrying ability. Jumping to conclusions, one might assume that this is the type most often attributed to the perfect woman. It could be. But I have two thoughts on that. First, these classifications are only further attempts to put women into categories. Either a woman is perfect or she is not, so if she is not, pinning on her a multitude of labels will not make her perfect. Secondly, I do not think categories are necessary. They may help one avoid pitfalls and understand what one may encounter in various women, but to eliminate these categories would not diminish a perfect woman in any way. If we must keep these categories, feeling that we would be lost without them, how does the perfect woman fit in here?

It is my opinion that the perfect woman would have a balance of all the four. She would not be dominant in any one, but able to use these as tools much like her psychological functions. She can be maternal when it is necessary. She can be independent when circumstances call for it and she can be a mediator when that is what she wants to be. But the pivot point would be the companion, the relationship oriented type revolving around Eros. Eros is the nature of the feminine soul and the other types only complement the basis of her nature in a well-balanced, whole, integrated personality. The perfect woman is what she wants to be, when she wants to be, and the key

word is "appropriate." She can relate through her nature using all the functions and tools available the same way a man should be able to relate to a woman through the appropriate anima image. There is no one best attitude or mode of dealing with life--flexibility and adaptability are essential.

Love,

    Father

July 29, 1954

Dearest Son,

A thought just crossed my mind. It is this: could you take an average everyday woman and make her into a perfect woman by training, education, analysis, etc.? I feel the answer is yes and no. Yes, to the degree that it is possible, and no, to the degree that it is an inherent quality. The first obvious argument that I wish to dispel is that of predestination--that if a woman is born to be perfect, nothing can stop her and, if not, nothing will ever let her be perfect. I counter that argument with free-will: if she wants to be perfect she will be. Somewhere within those two extremes we can search for the truth.

If you were to describe all the attributes of a perfect woman and then try to mold an average woman into perfection, would you succeed? Again, yes and no. If she is predisposed towards becoming perfect she will eventually get there either through guidance and the right conditions or through hard knocks and bitter experience. But if it is an inherent quality and she does not have it in her, then too bad. Then perfection can be said to be a gift, a talent, acquired at birth. That is why there are so few perfect women (or are they few in number?) just as there are so few musical geniuses. The argument there is reinforced by the question that if the little girl did not learn how to swing, can she learn now? I tend to think not; she cannot go back and relive her childhood, but she can learn new attitudes, develop new feelings and expand her level of consciousness.

Let us liken perfection to religion. There are many different religions with the same basic goal: getting to Heaven. Now that is very simplistic, but it does make a good analogy. If one lives right, follows the instructions of the religion, one will make it to Heaven. Likewise, I believe that perfection is akin to Heaven in that there are different ways to get there. The obvious is that some women are born with soul power. They start out towards perfection with intelligence, personality, everything right from birth. They come by it naturally and are the ones most often praised because at every step of the way they are perfect and it is recognized. The other way of reaching perfection is through developing it; by inner development and evolution. Most women reach it this way after a long, hard struggle towards self-realization. They are no less perfect when they achieve it than those who are born with it. If anything, theirs is more beautiful because it was cast in

the fire of suffering.

Now back to the question: can an average woman become perfect? If she wants to, she can work on it as a lifetime goal and maybe reach it. Some may be forced into it by circumstances. Some may be predisposed and eventually find the resources to get there. Some are born with it. Some are ignorant and could not care less. Some want to be very imperfect. The point is that if any woman wants to achieve it, the road is open to her, but it may be a tough road to travel. But no one is precluded from making the effort. Maybe it is easier than that, though. It may be that the seeds or germ of perfection is in everyone, dormantly waiting to have the opportunity to sprout to life. Maybe it is only the desire to become perfect that fertilizes that seed to grow. Maybe it is only an awareness that it does exist that sparks the imagination to make it happen. Maybe it is an ironic twist of fate that we are all closer to perfection than we realize and keep on searching all our lives to try to find something that is very easy to achieve, but we think it is difficult and thereby spend our time searching rather than working at it. Maybe the same could be said for love, happiness and peace.

Love,

Father

August 12, 1954

Dear Son,

Man has experienced the whole spectrum of woman in her various forms: wife, mother, lover, sister, aunt, daughter, witch, etc. Yet, all of this is encompassed by the anima who is an archetype of all femininity, not just one of the above forms. The Great Mother is the epitome of the archetypes--to encounter her, or any of them, would be a mind boggling and nearly impossible experience; it is beyond our comprehension. We can only envision her and speak objectively of her traits and qualities. You cannot experience her on a rational, human level. Yet, the anima is somewhat different. She partakes of the Great Mother and all the others so that in experiencing her, you are not encountering a specific archetype as such, but all of them at once and yet none of them specifically. She is a collage of all female archetypes in which all can be seen as representing each one, but not enough of each one is presented to enable you to discern the entire presence of the total archetype. I see in her a partial representation of my sister, my mother, my wife, my aunt, but not the archetype of the sister, wife, mother, etc.

At any one time, the anima can be any one of these partial forms which allows us to imagine the greater whole of what she is representing, but not enough to actually allow us to envision the true, total archetype. She then moves on to reveal another partial representative form of a female archetype, but not enough again to give rise to its true and uncomprehensible entity. She is the thread of femininity that ties all the female archetypes together and as such represents the entire spectrum of feminine archetypes through her representation of their common bond. She reveals only that portion of each that enables us to recognize the qualities that make each archetype specifically female--not any of the features that distinguish each one from the other as a complete, separate, total entity. She is like the breasts on an ancient statue whose face has been weathered away by Time. We do not know who the statue represents, but by recognizing the breasts, we know instinctively that it is a woman and our mind is free to imagine who she might have been representing without ever knowing for certain. The anima lets us see the breasts, brings them into awareness, but never reveals the faces that they belong to. Humans are not meant to gaze upon the faces of the archetypes and she has none to show us, only an endless array of faceless statues with breasts--all labeled mother, sister, wife, etc.

You do not encounter an archetype through the anima. She is only like a shadow in which you can recognize a female shape, and imagine some of the characteristics of the part she is playing, but as soon as that is almost grasped, the characteristics change. She is elusive enough that you cannot catch and hold her; therefore, the archetype is never fully perceived, only enough to give a clue and then it changes again to whatever fancies her next.

Actually, there is not enough in her to be able to discern another archetype as she would then be that other archetype. Therefore, she can only hint at what she wants us to see and can never completely follow through in revealing a full blown archetype. But it takes our careful attention as to her beckoning and a degree of imagination to cooperate in viewing this wide spectrum that she portrays of herself, divorced from any other archetype.

She hints at what archetype she is portraying, or more exactly she plays the part that she wants us to see by affecting our feelings. It is our own special set of feelings that are evoked as she hits the chord of feeling that corresponds to that image she wants us to perceive. We have a certain feeling that swells up inside when we hear the word "mother" or "wife" or "prostitute." She evokes those same feelings in harmony to the image she is representing and it is through that feeling that we think of the word mother, wife, or prostitute as the case may be. Therefore, the anima cannot represent the whole spectrum of feminine archetypes or images unless we have sufficient corresponding feelings to allow her to have access to our imagination. Without a full range of feelings, the anima is limited.

Love,

Father

August 24, 1954

My Dear Son,

I said before that possibly the perfect woman will turn out to be a divorcee. This is not a universal truth, but if the circumstances are right, the evolution is inevitable. That is because some may undergo what could be called "an initiation back to life." What is meant is not that they were not in life, but they got out of synch and had to find their way back onto track the hard way. The ordeal opened up the door to a new and better life because they came to a greater understanding of their own being.

I have often questioned if it is better for a woman to be sheltered from the realities of a divorce or for her to muddle through to experience its harsh realities. The answer is an individual one: for some it is better, for others not. "Sheltering" here means not having to go it alone--having time to reflect on her mistakes, but to have another person to guide her over such rough times--in short, finding a good new lover right away. Most do not have the benefits of having a loving, understanding person available. They must go to the gates of hell and back if they are to regain heaven. To put it another way, they have to wander in the wilderness just like Christ did. Only their "wandering" takes on a different form. They do not wander exactly, they rush. They rush into a realm of unknowing. For example, a woman who had the benefits of home and family suddenly finds herself single. The thought is frightening. She has been abandoned (by choice or circumstances) and is like an island cast adrift. How can she bring order back into her life?

Many are afraid and desperate. After much hesitation and doubt, they venture out to look for companionship and hopefully find a new mate. But the search through this avenue is precarious as they soon find out. All they encounter is the same type of people all looking for the same thing. The realization is stark. So the real love and companionship turns into an affair. The relationships developed usually are only physical and approach the verge of hopelessness: people reaching out for a life preserver only to find another reaching for the same thing. The activity may accelerate as she finds comfort in her new-found sexual freedom. But it is all an illusion and in time she pays the price. Soon, the law of psychic balance comes into play and the swing is in the other direction. So the cycle completes itself--the trek in the wilderness draws to a close with the onslaught of guilty feelings and depression. From being fearful, she had gone through a stage of sexual

liberation, all the way to guilt and depression. At this point, if she can come to her senses and realize that all this had been nonsense, she can go forth so much wiser. If she can just tell herself that all that thrashing about was not the real person she is and that she is worth more than all that, the experience will have gotten her out of the woods safely. Her life is now before her and how she lives it is up to her.

That is how some have to go through it to find themselves. Some are fortunate to have someone to keep them from ever wandering off into the wilderness. Some, however, wander off and never return. They are the unheralded ones because they are lost and will never be found. They fall victim to the animus, however negative he may appear. Their search leads them on a chase to find either a Father image or a real father for her children, or both. And in their desperation, they use sex as the only means to accomplish their goal. And so the merry-go-round spins on, all aboard trying to catch the brass ring. Some step off and remain dizzy all their lives; the fortunate few regain their sense of direction. And from those few, some may develop their full potential and unfold into a perfect woman...the hard way.

Love,

Father

September 9, 1954

My Very Dearest Son,

At last I see the sun dipping down behind the distant mountains that once held the promise of my quest. Weary, feet unable to go on another step, I set up my final camp. It is the end of the trail for now. Tonight I will sit around the fire and contemplate the experiences of many long years and maybe shed a tear in sadness for coming up empty-handed. But weary as I am, like the explorers and mountain men of old, I will be planning my next escapade. The old cliche that "there's no rest for the wicked" offers me a smile and a glimmer of hope. With this attempt, I have not failed, only strengthened my resolve to carry on further. I did start out a mite hastily this time around, not having the benefit of Wisdom or experience. But next time I will be starting out as a seasoned veteran in a campaign where every step is a step toward Truth and understanding.

Hopefully, with these letters I have instilled a sense of adventure in your imagination that will urge you to take up the quest also. If you do, you will soon realize that once begun it never ceases. You can never give up the quest, be it for the Holy Grail or the perfect woman. So, with this last letter, I must bid you fond adieu, my son, for I have nothing else to offer you except a memento that may provide some encouragement on the long journey you must undertake into the realm of both worlds. What I give you is a dream, one that I had many years ago. In it, I was sitting on the bank of a quiet river one night. The moonlight was reflecting off some object half buried in the ground a few feet from where I was sitting. I went over to it and discovered it to be a small metal box, very old. Expecting to find gold or some other treasure inside, I opened it and found only an old parchment. Disappointed, I took it over by the fire where I could barely make out the faded writing. It said: "Above all else, it is the anima who is perfect. Once you know her and have a good relationship with her, then you can search for the perfect outer woman because you will not be fooled, project the wrong things or have tricks played on you. You will then know all women by understanding the feminine element within yourself. You will have the guidance of your inner woman--her eyes can see the perfect outer woman. You will have a greater understanding, a better relationship with all women and will no longer be under their mystical, magical power. You will at last reach the conclusion that the perfect woman, the guardian angel, the keeper of the gate to the unconscious, the link with God, is all. The anima is the ultimate--your inner

queen and the real missing half of your long, lost soul. Once you realize this, you will then know the answer to the question: Whom does the grail serve? She serves you, if you serve Her!"

Love,

Your Wise Old Man

P.S. I've put together a list of books you might want to look at. They have helped me in my quest and may also give you greater insight.

The Psychology of CG Jung by Jolande Jacobi

Jung's Typology by Marie-Louise Von Franz and James Hillman

He: Understanding Masculine Psychology by Robert A. Johnson

She: Understanding Feminine Psychology by Robert A. Johnson

Animus and Anima by Emma Jung

The I and the Not I: A Study in the Development of Consciousness by M. Esther Harding

The Way of All Women by M. Esther Harding

The Feminine in Fairytales by Marie-Louise Von Franz